NORWEGIAN:
AN ESSENTIAL GRAMMAR

NORWEGIAN: AN ESSENTIAL GRAMMAR

Åse-Berit and Rolf Strandskogen
Translated by Barbara White

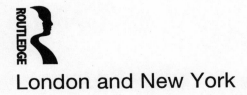

London and New York

First published in 1986
by Oris Forlag, Norway
Second edition 1989
Republished 1995
by Routledge
11 New Fetter Lane
London EC4P 4EE

Simultaneously published in the USA and Canada
by Routledge
29 West 35th Street
New York
NY 10001

© Oris Forlag, Norway 1986

Printed in Great Britain by
TJ Press (Padstow) Ltd, Cornwall

Printed on acid-free paper

British Library Cataloguing in Publication Data
A catalogue record for this book is available from the British Library

Library of Congress Cataloging in Publication Data
Strandskogen, Åse-Berit.
  [Norsk grammatikk for utlendinger. English]
  Norwegian: a practical grammar / Åse-Berit and Rolf Strandskogen;   translated by
Barbara White.
  Includes index.
  1. Norwegian language–Grammar. 2. Norwegian language–Textbooks for foreign
speakers–English. I. Strandskogen, Rolf. II. Title.
PD2623.S88 1994
439.8'282421–dc20
                                             93-45628
                                               CIP

ISBN 0–415–10979–5

Contents

3

4

Preface

This grammar has been written specially for non-Norwegians. Our aim has been to give a simple, step-by-step presentation of the grammatical rules and systems of Norwegian «bokmål», one of the two official written variants of Norwegian. The many examples given throughout the book assist the reader in practical usages which have proved difficult for those learning the language. As the intention of this book is to give a *practical* guide to modern Norwegian as it is used in an everyday context, emphasis has been given to providing translations of the Norwegian examples which are as colloquial and idiomatic as possible. The British English variants used throughout in the translations may on occasion appear unfamiliar to speakers of, for example, American English, but this should not be an obstacle to a full understanding of the text.

Haslum, January 1986

Åse-Berit and Rolf Strandskogen
Barbara White

I Parts of speech

In Norwegian, words are traditionally classified by these 10 parts of speech:

1. VERBS – examples: gå (go), lese (read), snakke (talk)
2. ARTICLES – examples: en, ei, et (a, one)
3. NOUNS – examples: hus (house), mat (food), bok (book)
4. ADJECTIVES – examples: god (good), stor (big), ung (young)
5. ADVERBS – examples: ute (out), hjemme (at home), nå (now)
6. PRONOUNS – examples: jeg (I), meg (me), min (my, mine)
7. CONJUNCTIONS – examples: hvis (if), fordi (because), og (and)
8. INTERJECTIONS – examples: au (ouch), hei (hello), uff (oh)
9. NUMERALS – examples: en (one), to (two), første (first), annen (second)
10. PREPOSITIONS – examples: til (to), på (on, at), hos (by, with)

VERBS

Infinitive

FORM:
Most infinitives end in a vowel, usually unstressed -e
Examples:

snakke (talk)	fortelle (tell)	gå (go)
reise (travel)	synge (sing)	bo (live)
spørre (ask)	danse (dance)	sy (sew)

Verbs ending in -s also have the -s form in the infinitive.
Examples:

trives (thrive, do well)	treffes (meet up)
møtes (meet each other)	brukes (be used)

Note: Verbs are always given in a dictionary in the infinitive form, often preceded by the infinitive marker *å* (to).

FUNCTION:
Infinitive form without «å»
a. After modal auxiliaries:
   Examples:
   Jeg kan *snakke* norsk. (I can *speak* Norwegian.)
   Han vil ikke *komme* nå. (He doesn't want to *come* now.)
   Du bør ikke *gjøre* det. (You shouldn't *do* that.)
   De skulle også *kjøpe* et hus. (They were also going to *buy* a house.)
   Dere må *spise* nå. (You must *eat* now.)
   Jeg tør ikke *gå* ute når det er mørkt. (I don't dare *walk* outside after dark.)

b. **After the verbs «be» (ask), «høre» (hear), «kjenne» (feel), «la» (let), «se» (see)**
Examples:
Jeg bad ham *komme.* (I asked him to *come.*)
Han lot oss *være sammen.* (He let us *be together.*)
Jeg hørte noen *snakke* der ute. (I heard someone *talking* out there.)
Jeg så dem *løpe* av sted i full fart. (I saw them *run* off at full speed.)
Jeg kjente såret *svi.* (I felt the cut *stinging.*)

c. **In such expressions as:**
Hvorfor *gråte* når man kan le? (Why *cry* when you can laugh?)
Hvorfor ikke *gjøre* det? (Why don't we *do* that?)
Nei, *snakke*, det kunne han ikke. (No, *talk* [was something] he couldn't do.)

d. **In a string of infinitives:**
See under Infinitive form with «å», section f.

Infinitive form with «å»
a. **As the subject of a sentence:**
Examples:
Å *snakke* norsk er litt vanskelig. (*Speaking* [literally: *to speak*] Norwegian is a bit difficult.)
Å *gå* på ski er morsomt. (*Skiing* [literally: *to walk on skis*] is fun.)
Å *tale* er sølv, men å *tie* er gull. (Speech is silver, but silence is golden [literally: *to speak* is silver, but *to remain silent* is golden].)

b. **As the object of a sentence:**
Examples:
Jeg liker å *danse.* (I like *to dance.*)
Han ønsket å *fly.* (He wanted *to fly.*)
Hun prøvde å *snakke.* (She tried *to talk.*)

c. **As the complement of a sentence:**
Examples:
Det er å *gjøre* for mye av ingenting. (That is *making* [literally: *to make*] too much out of nothing.)
Det synes å *ta* lang tid. (It seems *to be taking* [literally: *to take*] a long time.)

d. **In infinitive clauses:**

Examples:

Jeg har mye *å fortelle* fra den reisen. (I have a lot *to tell* from that trip.)

Han ville gjerne ha noe *å drikke*. (He would like something *to drink*.)

Det var ikke annet *å gjøre*. (There was nothing else *to do*.)

e. **After a preposition:**

Examples:

Hun gikk for *å handle*. (She went out *shopping*.)

Det var et forsøk på *å lure* de andre. (It was an attempt *to fool* the others.)

De hadde bestemt seg for *å gjøre* det. (They had decided *to do* it.)

f. **In a string of infinitives:**

1. **Coordinated infinitives: Å is usually omitted after *og* (and) and *eller* (or).**

   Examples:

   Han lærte å snakke og (å) skrive. (He learned to talk and (to) write.)

   De likte å hoppe og (å) danse. (They liked to jump and (to) dance.)

   De skulle begynne å skrive eller (å) lese. (They were going to start to write or (to) read.)

2. **Uncoordinated infinitives: Å cannot be omitted.**

   Examples:

   Han må lære å snakke. (He must learn to talk.)

        ↑   ↑
       inf.   inf.

   Han må lære å snakke, (å) skrive og (å) lese.

      ↑   ↑   ↑   ↑
     inf.   inf.   inf.   inf.

   These 2 infinitives   These 2 infinitives
   are uncoordinated   are coordinated

   (He must learn to talk, (to) write and (to) read.)

Hun hadde bestemt seg for å prøve å slutte å røyke og drikke.

$\uparrow$ inf. $\uparrow$ inf. $\uparrow$ inf. $\uparrow$ ınf.

These 2 infinitives are uncoordinated   These 2 infinitives are coordinated

(She had decided to try to stop smoking and drinking.)

g. **In such expressions as:**
Sant *å si* (To tell the truth)
Vel *å merke* (Mind you)
Så *å si* (So to speak)

h. **After *Vær så snill* (please):**
Examples:

Vær så snill *å lukke* døra!
(Please *shut* the door!)

Or: Vær så snill *og lukk* døra!

Vær så snill *å komme* presis!

(Please *come* on time!)

Or: Vær så snill *og kom* presis!

Vær så snill *å forsyne* dere!»

(Please *help* yourselves!)

Or: Vær så snill *og forsyn* dere!

i. **After an imperative:**
Husk *å slukke* lyset! (Remember *to switch off* the light!)
Prøv *å forstå* dette! (Try *to understand* this!)
Begynn *å gå* nå! (Start *walking* now!)

Imperative

FORM:
Verbs ending in -e in the infinitive lose the -e to form the imperative.
Examples:

Infinitive:		*Imperative:*
snakke (talk)	$\longrightarrow$	snakk! (talk!)
spise (eat)	$\longrightarrow$	spis! (eat!)
komme (come)	$\longrightarrow$	kom! (come!)
		(NB **m** is never written double when final.)

For verbs which do not end in -e in the infinitive, the form of the imperative is identical to that of the infinitive.

Examples:

gå (go) $\longrightarrow$ gå! (go!)

si (say) $\longrightarrow$ si! (say!)

Negative imperative

Examples:

Ikke snakk! (Don't talk!)

Ikke kom! (Don't come!)

Ikke røyk! (Don't smoke!)

Ikke gå! (Don't go!)

FUNCTION:

The imperative can be used to give an order. As the imperative form can often be regarded as a command, a milder, more polite form of expression is frequently used in order to avoid being too harsh or direct.

Examples:

Skriv dette brevet! $\longrightarrow$ Vil du skrive dette brevet?

(Write this letter!) (Will you write this letter?)

Gå nå! $\longrightarrow$ Vær så snill å gå nå.

(Go now!) (Please go now.)

or:

Kan du gå nå?

(Can you go now?)

Hent pakkene på postkontoret! $\longrightarrow$ Kunne du (være så snill å) hente pakkene på postkontoret?

(Pick up the parcels at the post office!) (Could you (please) pick up the parcels at the post office?)

Using the imperative does not always have to give a harsh impression – a lot depends on the way it is said (intonation, stress patterns, etc.). The imperative is given a friendly tone when followed by *så, da vel*, etc.

Examples:

Kom så tar vi en kopp kaffe! (Come on, let's have a cup of coffee!)

Sett deg da vel! (Do sit down then!)

Gjør det da (vel)! ((Well), do it then!)

Subjunctive

FORM:
As the infinitive.

FUNCTION:
There are few examples of the subjunctive in modern Norwegian, compared to Old Norse where the subjunctive form of the verb was in regular use.
Modern Norwegian does however use the subjunctive in certain idioms.
Examples:
Kongen *leve!* (Long live the King!)
Enhver *feie* for sin egen dør! ([Literally: let every man sweep before his own door!], i.e. put your own house in order)
In Old Norse, the subjunctive was used to express a wish, request or intent. Nowadays other forms are used, such as the conditional tense, modal verbs, etc.

Indicative

In all the indicative tenses the appropriate inflectional endings are joined on to the verb stem. The ending for each tense is the same for all persons of the verb, both singular and plural.

In the indicative these forms of the verb are found:

ACTIVE

1. *Present:* Han *spiser* (He eats)
2. *Past (Imperfect):* Han *spiste* (He ate)
3. *Perfect:* Han *har spist* (He has eaten)
4. *Pluperfect:* Han *hadde spist* (He had eaten)
5. *Future:* Han *skal spise* (He will eat)
6. *Future perfect:* Han *skal ha spist* (He will have eaten)
7. *Conditional:* Han *skulle spise* (He was going to/about to eat)
8. *Conditional perfect:* Han *skulle (ha) spist* (He should have eaten)

17

PASSIVE

1. *Present:* Maten *blir spist* / Maten *spises*
   (The food is being eaten / The food is eaten)
2. *Past:* Maten *ble spist* / Maten *spistes*
   (The food was being eaten / The food was eaten)
3. *Perfect:* Maten *har blitt spist*
   Maten *er blitt spist*
   Maten *er spist*
   (The food has been eaten)
4. *Pluperfect:* Maten *hadde blitt spist*
   Maten *var blitt spist*
   (The food had been eaten)
5. *Future:* Maten *skal spises* / Maten *skal bli spist*
   (The food will be eaten)
6. *Future perfect:* Maten *skal ha blitt spist*
   (The food will have been eaten)
7. *Conditional:* Maten *skulle spises* / Maten *skulle bli spist*
   (The food was to / about to be eaten)
8. *Conditional perfect:* Maten *skulle (ha) blitt spist*
   (The food should have been eaten)

More about the passive: see the section on Verbs ending in -s.

Present

FORM:
Infinitive + r: Examples: *snakker* (speak), *går* (go)
Exception:
a. spør (ask), gjør (do), vet (know), sier (say), er (am), etc.
b. verbs ending in -s: spises (is eaten), synes (think), møtes (meet each other), etc.
c. modal auxiliaries: vil (will), skal (shall), må (must), kan (can), bør (ought), tør (dare).

FUNCTION:
a. **The present tense is used about something that is happening at the present moment.**
   Examples:
   Barnet *sover* nå. (The child is sleeping now.)
   De *bor* i Norge nå. (They live in Norway now.)

Sometimes two verbs in the present tense can be combined to express an event of a certain duration which is taking place at the present time. (See the section on the Continuous aspect.)
Examples:
Han *sitter* og *skriver*. (He sits and writes, ie. he is sitting writing.)
Hun *ligger* og *sover*. (She lies and sleeps, ie. she is lying sleeping.)
De *står* og *prater*. (They stand and talk, ie. they are standing talking.)

b. **Eternal truths:**
Examples:
To og to *er* fire. (Two and two are four.)
Vann *koker* ved 100 °C. (Water boils at 100 °C.)

c. **Habitual statements:**
Example:
Hver sommer *reiser* vi til utlandet. (Every summer we go abroad.)

d. **With future time reference, especially in connection with temporal adverbs:**
Example:
I morgen *reiser* vi. (We are leaving tomorrow.)

e. **In commands:**
Example:
Nå *tier* du stille! (Be quiet now!)
Here the imperative is used just as often: *Ti* stille!

f. **Historical present, giving a narrative more excitement and bringing it alive:**
Example:
Han satt og leste i avisa. Plutselig *kommer* det noen. (He was sitting reading the paper. Suddenly someone comes.)

Past (imperfect)

FORM:

a. **Regular verbs:** The verb stem + -et or -de/-te/-dde

å kaste	kast	+ et	→	kastet
(to throw)				
å leve	lev	+ de	→	levde
(to live)				
å lyse	lys	+ te	→	lyste
(to shine)				
å bo	bo	+ dde	→	bodde
(to live)				

(See the section on Regular verbs, page 00.)

b. **Irregular verbs:** Vowel change

å gå	→	gikk
(to go)		
å synge	→	sang
(to sing)		
å ligge	→	lå
(to lie)		

(See the list of irregular verbs on page 41.)

FUNCTION:

a. **The past, or imperfect, tense refers to an event which happened at a given time in the past.**
Example:
Han *var* her i går. (He was here yesterday.)

In questions beginning with «Når . . .?» (When) the past tense is used when referring to a period or time before the present.
Example:
Når *kom* du til Norge? (When did you come to Norway?)

b. Habitual past.
Example:
Han *gikk* hver dag til kontoret. (He walked to the office every day.)

c. The past is often used to express a spontaneous feeling, emotion or sensation in the present.
Example:
(Hun smaker på kaka og sier:) Det *var* deilig kake! (She tastes the cake and says: This is a lovely cake!)

d. The past can be used to refer to the future – see the section about the conditional.

Perfect

FORM:
Auxiliary + past participle
har   *spist*

Sometimes the auxiliary «er» is used instead of «har». Example:
Han *er* reist. (He *has* left.)
«Er» is often used in conjunction with verbs of motion and with verbs which denote a transition from one state to another.
Example:
reise (go, leave), gå (go, walk), sovne (fall asleep), visne (wither)
«Han *har* reist» (he has left) denotes the action itself, while
«Han *er* reist» indicates the result of the action: he is no longer here.

In modern Norwegian *har* as the auxiliary is becoming more and more widespread in all contexts.

FUNCTION:
a. Han *har spist.* (He has eaten.)
   The perfect tense is used to express an event which happened in the past, without fixing it in time. (When referring to a specific point in time, the past tense is used: «Han *spiste* klokka to.» (He ate at two o'clock.))

b. Han *har vært* her i to måneder. (He has been here for two months.)
   The use of the perfect tense here denotes that he has been here for a certain period of time, but gives no indication of *when* that period was. He may still be here, or he may have been here several years ago.

21

In questions beginning with «Hvor lenge / Hvor lang tid?» (How long?) distinguish between:

1. the use of the perfect tense, where the main interest lies in the duration of the event rather than an exact point in time.
   Example:
   Hvor lenge *har* du *vært* i Norge? (How long have you been in Norway?),
   ie. you are still there, or you have been there for a while,

   and:

2. the use of the past (imperfect) tense if the event's duration is irrelevant.
   Example:
   Hvor lenge *var* du i Norge (i 1970)? (How long were you in Norway (in 1970)?),
   ie. you are no longer there.

c. Når du *har lært* norsk, kan du få en jobb. (When you have learnt Norwegian, you can get a job.)

NOW	RESULT	FUTURE
Du lærer norsk (You learn Norwegian)	Du har lært norsk (You have learnt Norwegian)	Du kan få en jobb (You can get a job)

The perfect tense here indicates that an event must have a result in the future (learn Norwegian) so that another event can follow (get a job).

Pluperfect

FORM:
Auxiliary + past participle
hadde   spist

(The use of the auxiliary *var* (past tense of «er») in the formation of the pluperfect follows the same rules as «er» in the perfect tense.)

FUNCTION:

a. Etter at vi *hadde spist,* gikk vi på kino. (After we had eaten we went to the cinema.)

The pluperfect denotes an event in the past («vi hadde spist») which preceded another event also in the past («vi gikk på kino»).

b. *Hadde* jeg *hatt* tid, $\begin{cases} \text{hadde jeg hjulpet deg.} \\ \text{skulle jeg ha hjulpet deg.} \end{cases}$

Dersom jeg *hadde hatt* tid, skulle jeg ha hjulpet deg. (If I had had time I would have helped you.)
Bare han *hadde kommet.* (If only he had come.)
The pluperfect is often used to express an unfulfilled wish.

Future

FORM:

Auxiliary	+	infinitive
skal/vil		*spise*
kommer til		*å spise*

FUNCTION:
Future time can be expressed in several ways in Norwegian: using «skal» (shall), «vil» (will), «kommer til å» (going to) and by using the present tense of the verb.

Skal is used when the future event is within the speaker's control.
Examples:
Jeg *skal skrive* et brev til tanten min. (I shall write a letter to my aunt.)
De *skal reise* til Italia på ferie til sommeren. (They will go to Italy on holiday this summer.)

Vil is used when it is assumed that an event will happen, but over which one has no control.
Examples:
Oljeprisen *vil* snart *gå* ned. (The price of oil will soon drop.)
De *vil* nok *like seg* i Norge. (They will be sure to like it in Norway.)

23

The use of «vil» in these examples indicates an uncertainty about something one cannot influence, but one is reasonably sure about the outcome.

A useful rule of thumb is that, if the sentence can be preceded by «jeg regner med at . . .» (I assume that . . .) then the correct verb to use is «vil»:

Ekspertene regner med at oljeprisen vil gå ned. (The experts assume that the price of oil will drop.)

Kommer til å is a less formal alternative to «vil». It is very commonly used in spoken Norwegian, and is used instead of «vil» where it is natural to use an informal tone.

Examples:
De *kommer til å* like seg i Norge. (They are going to like it in Norway.)
Du *kommer til å* bli syk hvis du går ut uten jakke. (You are going to get ill if you go out without a jacket.)

Sometimes «kommer til å» can be replaced by a verb in the present tense, which is then normally accompanied by a modifying adverbial phrase.

Examples:
Han *våkner* sikkert snart.
Han *kommer* sikkert *til å våkne* snart.
(I'm sure he's going to wake up soon.)

Han *spiser* nok maten når han blir sulten.
Han *kommer* nok *til å spise* maten når han blir sulten.
(No doubt he will eat his food when he gets hungry.)

The present tense is very often used in Norwegian to express future time, usually in conjunction with an adverbial phrase of time. This usage has its parallel in English.

Examples:
Jeg *reiser* i morgen. (I am leaving tomorrow.)
It is also possible, though less common, to say:
Jeg *skal* reise i morgen. (I shall leave tomorrow.)

24

Further examples:

Byggearbeidet *begynner* en gang i neste uke. (The building work starts some time next week.)

Jeg *sender* brevet i morgen. (I'll send the letter tomorrow.)

In temporal clauses, the present tense is most often used:

Når du *kommer*, skal vi spise. (When you come we will eat.)

Wrong: Når du skal komme

Når vi *er* ferdig, kan vi ta en kopp te. (When we are finished we can have a cup of tea.)

Wrong: Når vi skal/vil bli ferdig . . .

The present tense is also usual in conditional clauses:

Hvis du *arbeider* hardt, vil du klare det. (If you work hard you will manage it.)

Wrong: Hvis du skal arbeide hardt, vil du klare det.

However, in certain conditional clauses, the present tense cannot be used.

Examples:

Hvis du *skal lære* norsk, må du gå på kurs. (If you are going to learn Norwegian, you have to take a course.)

Hvis du *skal bli med* til byen, må du først gjøre leksene dine. (If you are going to come to town with me, you have to do your homework first.)

As the examples show, this use of «skal» corresponds to a large extent to the English «be going to», meaning «have the intention of». The requirement expressed in the main clause has to be satisfied before the intention in the conditional clause can be realized.

Note that the verb «bli» (be, become) is nearly always expressed in the future as «vil bli», «kommer til å bli» or «blir»:

De *vil bli* glad for å treffe dere. ⎫
De *kommer til å bli* glad for å treffe dere. ⎬ (They will be happy
De *blir* glad for å treffe dere. ⎭ to meet you.)

Future perfect

FORM:
Auxiliary + ha + past participle
skal/vil   ha   spist

FUNCTION:
Han *skal ha spist* før programmet begynner. (He will have eaten before/by the time the programme starts.)

---

7 a.m.	Now
8 a.m.	He is eating
9 a.m.	The programme starts

The future perfect tense denotes an action or event in the future which will be over by the time another action or event occurs.

Note: «Han skal ha spist» can also mean «He is presumed to have eaten».

Conditional

FORM:
Auxiliary + infinitive
skulle/ville   spise

FUNCTION:
a. Han *skulle spise* da jeg kom. (He was about to eat when I came.)
   The conditional tense denotes the future from an orientation in
   the past.

b. Jeg *skulle ønske* han kom snart. (I wish he would come soon.)
   The conditional is often used to convey a wish or hope which
   may possibly be realized. In various other languages the
   subjunctive is often used in this context.

   Note the use of the past tense in the clause following the
   conditional verb, even though the reference is to the future.

   See also the chapter on Modal auxiliaries.

26

Conditional perfect

FORM:
Auxiliary + (ha) + past participle
skulle/ville   *(ha)*   *spist*

FUNCTION:
a. Jeg *skulle (ha) reparert* bilen før ferien begynte. (I should have repaired the car before the holidays started.)
The conditional perfect tense is used to express something which should have been done, but hasn't. (You regret not repairing the car before the holidays.) The fact that it is now too late is shown by the past tense of the verb in the second clause («begynte»).

b. Jeg *skulle (ha) reparert* bilen før ferien begynner. (I should repair the car before the holidays start.)
It's still not too late, as the present tense of the second main verb shows («begynner»). The conditional perfect indicates something that should be done before something else.

c. Jeg *skulle* gjerne *(ha) snakket* med henne. (I would like to talk to her.)

The conditional tenses are frequently used to make a polite, respectful request. A more direct form of making the same request is «Jeg *vil* gjerne *snakke* med henne», but the conditional and conditional perfect in this context is normally to be preferred.

See also the chapter on Modal auxiliaries.

The continuous aspect

There are very few parallels in Norwegian for the English «-ing» expressing the continuous aspect. Whereas in English the present participle is the most common way to express continuation with verbs of duration (he was runn*ing,* she is read*ing,* etc.), in Norwegian the present participle is not used in this way.

Wrong: Han var løpende, hun var lesende

The correct forms are «Hun leser» or «Hun sitter og leser» (She is

reading), «Han løp» (He was running; also: he ran, depending on context).
In addition, Norwegian has other special devices to express duration when the emphasis is on a specific activity in progress:
– *holde på med å:*
Han holder på med å male huset akkurat nå. (He is painting the house right now.)
– *drive og:*
Hun drev og reparerte bilen da han kom. (She was in the process of/in the throes of repairing the car when he arrived.)

Certain verbs like «sitte», «ligge» and «stå» (sit, lie, stand) can also be combined with other verbs to express duration.
Examples:
Han *sitter og skriver* brev. (He is sitting writing letters.)
Jeg *lå og leste* avisen (I was lying reading the paper.)
De *hadde stått og pratet* i timesvis. (They had stood chatting for hours.)

Sequence of tenses

The tense of the verb usually changes from direct to indirect speech.

Direct speech:
PRESENT
Jeg *liker* meg her
(I like it here)

Indirect speech:
PAST (IMPERFECT)
Han *sa* at han *likte* seg her
(He said that he liked it here)

PAST
Jeg *gikk* en tur
(I went for a walk)

PLUPERFECT
Hun *sa* at hun *hadde gått* en tur
(She said she had been for a walk)

PERFECT
Jeg *har gått* en tur
(I have been for a walk)

PLUPERFECT
Hun *sa* hun *hadde gått* en tur
(She said she had been for a walk)

FUTURE
Vi *skal reise* i morgen
(We shall leave tomorrow)

CONDITIONAL
De *sa* at de *skulle reise* i morgen
(They said they were going to leave tomorrow)

28

In Old Norse the subjunctive was used in indirect speech, but in modern Norwegian the indicative mood is used throughout.

Modal auxiliaries

Skal (shall), *vil* (will), *kan* (can), *må* (must), *bør* (ought), *tør* (dare), *får* (may) [in some cases] form the class of modal auxiliaries. *Skal/vil* is used as the auxiliary in the formation of the future and conditional tenses. In general the modal auxiliaries express doubt, intention, recommendation, commands, etc., comparable to the use of the subjunctive in other languages. The imperfect forms of the modal auxiliaries often denote caution, politeness etc. rather than a direct reference to past time.

1. **Skal/skulle** (shall/should)
    «Skal» can be used to express the following:
    a. a command, order or demand:
        Jeg vil at du *skal gå.* (I want you to go.)
        Dere *skal gjøre* dette arbeidet! (You are going to do this work!)

    b. doubt or uncertainty:
        Skal jeg *spørre* henne nå? (Shall I ask her now?)
        Skal vi ta te eller kaffe? (Shall we have tea or coffee?)

    c. a threat:
        Hvis du ikke kommer med en gang, *skal* du *få* juling. (If you don't come at once, you'll get a beating.)
        Hvis dere sier noe, *skal* vi *drepe* dere. (If you say anything, we'll kill you.)

    d. a promise:
        Hvis du kommer hit, *skal* jeg *hjelpe* deg. (If you come here, I'll help you.)
        Hvis du er snill, *skal* du *få* sjokolade. (If you are good, you'll get some chocolate.)

    e. a rumour or supposition:
        Hun *skal* visst *være* i byen. (She is said to be in town.)
        Det *skal være* god mat der, har jeg hørt. (The food is supposed to be good there, I've heard.)

Note that in c and e, and to a certain extent in d above, the present tense of the verb can also be used.

«Skulle» is often used in conjunction with adverbs such as «heller» (better), «helst» (preferably), «nok» (probably, indeed), etc. in the context of giving advice or recommendation.
Examples:
Du *skulle* heller gjøre det. (You had better do it.)
Den boka *skulle* du lese – den er virkelig god. (You should read that book – it's really good.)
Hun *skulle* helst spise opp all maten sin. (She really ought to eat up all her food.)

«Skulle» can also be used in sentences denoting present time to express uncertainty or doubt. The tone becomes rather more cautious and polite than if «skal» is used.
Examples:
Skulle det *være* en kopp kaffe til? (May I offer you another cup of coffee?)
Skulle vi *gå* nå kanskje? (Should we go now, maybe?)

In both these examples, «skal» would also be correct.

2. **Vil/ville** (will/would)
«Vil/ville» often expresses willingness or desire, with a person as the subject.
Examples:
Jeg *vil* gjerne *reise* nå. (I wish to leave now.)
Vi *vil hjelpe* dere så godt vi kan. (We want to help you as best we can.)
Han *vil* at vi skal komme. (He wants us to come.)
Han *ville* at vi skulle komme. (He wanted us to come.)

Wrong: Han vil at jeg kommer. Han ville at jeg kom.

In the same way as «skulle», «ville» can also be used in present time to express caution and politeness:
Examples:
Jeg *ville* gjerne *snakke* med direktøren nå hvis det var mulig. (I would like to speak to the director now, if it was possible.)
Kanskje De *ville forsøke* en gang til? (Perhaps you would like to try again?)

3. **Må/måtte** (must/had to)
   denotes necessity.
   Examples:
   Du *må* gå selv om du ikke vil. (You must go, even if you don't want to.)
   Jeg *må* se den filmen. (I must see that film.)

   In certain expressions «må/måtte» can be used to express a hope or wish.
   Examples:
   Måtte lykken følge deg! (May luck be with you!)
   Må du ha det bra! (I wish you well.)

4. **Kan/kunne** (can/could)
   denotes ability, being able or capable of doing something or knowing how to.
   Examples:
   Hun *kan* norsk. (She knows Norwegian.) ie. understands, speaks and maybe writes Norwegian.
   Jeg *kan* lage mat. (I can cook.) ie. I know how to cook.

   «Kan/kunne» can also be used to give or ask permission to do something.
   Examples:
   Kan jeg røyke her? (May I smoke here?) ie. is it permitted for me to smoke here?
   Du *kan* røyke her. (You may smoke here.) ie. you are allowed to smoke here.

   «Kunne» sometimes gives the impression of restraint or caution.
   Examples:
   Kunne du hjelpe meg litt? (Could you help me a little?) instead of *Kan* du hjelpe . . . (Can you help . . .)
   Du *kunne* jo gjøre det på denne måten. (You could do it this way) instead of Du *kan* jo . . . (You can . . .)

   «Kunne» is used in unfulfilled wishes.
   Examples:
   Kunne jeg bare vinne noen penger. (If only I could win some money.)
   Bare han *kunne* komme snart. (If only he could come soon.)

5. **Får/fikk** (may/might)

can sometimes be used instead of «kan/kunne» to express permission.

Examples:

Får jeg gå nå? (May I go now?) ie. can I go now / is it in order for me to go now?

Du *får* gjøre det. (You may do that.) ie. you have permission to do that.

Fikk du gå nå? (Were you allowed to go now?)

Vi *får* snakke med dem i kveld. (Either: We may speak to them this evening, or: Let us speak to them this evening.)

Får/fikk followed by a past participle usually conveys the meaning of to manage or achieve something.

Examples:

Jeg *fikk* snakket med henne. (I managed to talk to her.)

Du *fikk* gjort mye i helgen. (You managed to do a lot at the weekend.)

Tror du at du *får* gjort det i kveld? (Do you think you'll manage to do it this evening?)

6. **Bør/burde** (ought to, should)

is used to give advice or a suggestion, rather than a command.

Examples:

Du *bør* gå nå. (You should/ought to go now.)

Du *burde* prøve. (You ought to try.)

7. **Tør/torde** (dare)

expresses boldness or courage.

Examples:

Jeg *tør* ikke si det. (I don't dare say it.)

Han *torde* ikke hoppe i vannet for han var redd det var kaldt. (He didn't dare jump into the water as he was afraid it was cold.)

Modal auxiliaries used without a main verb

Modal auxiliaries can occur in contexts where the main verb is omitted.

Examples:

Hvor *skal* du? (Where are you going?)

Jeg *skal* til byen. (I'm going to town.)

Hva *skal* du? (What are you going to do?)
Jeg *må* hjem. (I must go home.)
Jeg *vil* til Italia. (I want to go to Italy.)

How does one know which main verb has been left out?
In questions beginning with «Hvor?» (Where?), the verb is always
one of motion towards a place, e.g. go, travel, drive, etc. In many
cases an adverb will also give an additional clue, such as in
Jeg skal hjem. (I'm going home.)
where the meaning of «motion towards home» is contained in the
adverb *home*.
Questions beginning with «Hva?» (What?) always imply the verb
«do».

The main verb can only be omitted in questions beginning with:

Hvor (Where): Hvor skal du? (Where are you going?)
Hva (What): Hva skal du? (What are you going to do?)
Hvorfor (Why): Hvorfor skal du dit? (Why are you going there?)

Wrong: Hvordan skal du til Italia? Hvor lenge skal du i Italia?

Questions beginning with «Hvorfor» must also contain an adverb
of place which implies motion, such as «dit» (there, literally thence),
«hjem» (home), «bort» (away), etc.

Transitive and intransitive verbs

Examples:
Transitive: Høna *legger* egg. (The hen lays eggs.)
Intransitive: Høna *ligger* på egg. (The hen lies on eggs.)

TRANSITIVE VERBS
are verbs which can take a direct object.
Examples:

            direct object
                ↓
Han *spiser* et eple. (He eats an apple.)
    ↑
  trans. verb

direct object
↓
Hun *setter* glasset på bordet. (She puts the glass on the table.)
↑
trans. verb

INTRANSITIVE VERBS
are verbs which cannot take a direct object.
Examples:
Han *kommer* i morgen. (He is coming tomorrow.)
↑
intrans. verb

De *sitter* på kjøkkenet. (They are sitting in the kitchen.)
↑
intrans. verb

CONJUGATION OF SOME INTRANSITIVE AND TRANSITIVE VERBS
In many cases it is important to know the difference between
transitive and intransitive verbs. These are some of the most
common pairs of verbs:

Intransitive verbs:

Infinitive	Present	Past	Perfect
å ligge (to lie)	ligger	lå	ligget
å sitte (to sit)	sitter	satt	sittet
å henge (to hang)	henger	hang	hengt
å slenge (to dangle, hang around)	slenger	slang	slengt
å rekke (to reach)	rekker	rakk	rukket

Examples:
Han *lå* hele dagen. (He lay, = stayed in bed, all day.)
De har *sittet* og snakket i to timer nå. (They have been sitting talking
for two hours now.)
Jakka hans *hang* i gangen. (His jacket was hanging in the hall.)
De gikk og *slang* i gatene hele kvelden. (They hung around the streets
all evening.)
Juletreet *rakk* helt i taket. (The Christmas tree reached right up to the
ceiling.)

Note also: Han *rakk* ikke bussen. (He didn't catch the bus, ie. he
missed the bus.)

34

Transitive verbs:

Infinitive	Present	Past	Perfect
å legge (to lay, put)	legger	la	lagt
å sette (to set, place, put)	setter	satte	satt
å henge (to hang up)	henger	hengte	hengt
å slenge (to throw)	slenger	slengte	slengt
å rekke (to reach, pass)	rekker	rakte	rakt

Examples:
Hun *la* boka på bordet. (She put the book on the table.)
Han har *satt* blomstene i vasen. (He has put the flowers in the vase.)
Han *hengte* jakka si i gangen. (He hung his jacket up in the hall.)
Hun *slengte* klærne på gulvet. (She threw her clothes on the floor.)
Han *rakte* meg hånden sin. (He offered me his hand.)

Separable and inseparable compound verbs

a. **Many compound verbs are composed of an adverb or preposition plus a verb.**
   Examples:
   å utgå (to be omitted)   å tilby (to offer)
   å avtale (to arrange)   å oversette (to translate)
   å medbringe (to bring along) å oppfylle (to fulfil)

   These verbs are all *inseparable* compounds.

b. **In those instances where the adverb or preposition follows the verb, the compound is separable.**
   Examples:
   å dele ut (to hand out)   å sette over (to put on)
   å ta over (to take over)   å fylle opp (to fill up)
   å bringe med (to bring with)

c. **Choosing between separable and inseparable compounds.**
   Sometimes one can choose freely between the separable and the inseparable form of a compound verb. In everyday spoken Norwegian the separable form is most common.

Examples:

Teksten *omhandler* det nye lovforslaget. (The text is about the new Bill.)

Boka *handler om* kvinner. (The book is about women.)

Arbeiderne ble *oppsagt* uten forvarsel. (The workers were fired without warning.)

Vi ble *sagt opp* på dagen. (We were fired there and then.)

d. **Some compound verbs only have an inseparable form.**
   Examples:

å innrede (to fit out)	å oppdage (to discover)
å undervise (to teach)	å utgjøre (to comprise)
å gjenreise (to reconstruct)	å avtale (to arrange)

e. **Some compound verbs only have a separable form:**
   Examples:

   å kaste bort (to waste)
   å slite ut (to wear out)
   å si opp (to fire, resign)

f. **The separable and inseparable pairs of some compound verbs can have quite different meanings, where the inseparable form is often more abstract.**
   Examples:

oppdra: Han *oppdro* sine barn på en fornuftig måte. (He brought up his children in a sensible way.)

dra opp: Han *dro opp* korken på flasken. (He pulled the cork out of the bottle.)

gjengi: Han kunne *gjengi* hele samtalen. (He could quote the entire conversation.)

gi igjen: Kan du *gi* meg *igjen* på 100 kroner? (Can you give me change of 100 kroner?)

oversette: Han *oversatte* boka fra polsk til norsk. (He translated the book from Polish to Norwegian.)

sette over: Han *satte over* kaffekjelen. (He put the coffee on.)

As no rules exist for the choice of the correct form of compound verbs, each must be memorized individually.

g. **When compound verbs are used adjectivally or nominally they are always inseparable.**
Examples:
et innbetalt gebyr (a paid fee)
bortkastet tid (wasted time)
et opplyst rom (an illuminated room)
en utslitt genser (a worn-out sweater)
en oppsagt (a person who has been fired)
en innsatt (a prisoner, literally a person who has been put inside)

Present participle

FORM:
The present participle always ends in «-ende».
Examples:
syngende (singing), *sovende* (sleeping), *kjørende* (driving), *gående* (walking)

FUNCTION:
a. **The present participle does not occur very frequently in Norwegian. One of its main uses is as an adjective.**
Example:
et *sovende* barn (a sleeping child)

b. **It can also be used in conjunction with a main verb to describe an action of the subject.**
Example:
Han kom *syngende* inn i rommet. (He came into the room singing.)

c. **The present participle can also be used as an adverb which intensifies an adjective.**
Example:
skinnende rein (spotlessly clean, literally: shining clean)

d. **The present participle of verbs such as «sitte» (sit), «stå» (stand) and «ligge» (lie) are often used in conjunction with the verb «bli» (be) to denote an event of a certain duration.**
Examples:
Han *ble sittende* og prate. (He sat talking.)

Han *ble liggende* og tenke hele natta. (He lay thinking all night.)

Note that the second verb in this construction is always in the infinitive form.

e. **In some cases the present participle can be used as a noun.**
Examples:
De *reisende* måtte bytte tog. (The passengers (literally: those travelling) had to change trains.)
De *forbipasserende* la ikke merke til henne. (The passers-by did not notice her.)

Note that the present participle, although used here as a noun, does not inflect for number or gender.

Verbs ending in -s

These are verbs which end in -s in the infinitive. There are several different categories:

1. **Passive:**
   å brukes = å bli brukt (to be used)

2. **Active:**
   å trives (to be happy, thrive)

3. **Reciprocal:**
   å møtes = å møte hverandre (to meet each other)

4. **Reflexive:**
   å undres = å undre seg (to wonder, be surprised)

The conjugation of some of the most common verbs ending in -s follows. The numbers in brackets refer to the above categories.

Infinitive	Present	Past
finnes (2) (to exist, occur)	finnes/fins	fantes/fans
følges (1) (to be followed)	følges	fulgtes
høres (1,2) (be heard, to sound)	høres	hørtes
kjennes (2) (to feel)	kjennes	kjentes

lykkes (2) (to succeed)	lykkes	lyktes
minnes (2) (to recall)	minnes	mintes
møtes (1,3) (to be met, meet each other)	møtes	møttes
se(e)s (1,3) (to be seen, see each other)	se(e)s	så(e)s
slåss (3) (to fight)	slåss	sloss
spørres (1) (to depend, be asked)	spørs	spurtes
synes (2) (to seem)	synes	syntes
trives (2) (to be happy)	trives	trivdes
undres (4) (to wonder)	undres	undres

The verbs ending in -s are often irregular and are seldom used in tenses other than the present, which is identical to the infinitive form. The perfect forms of these verbs are not included here as the perfect tense is usually formed using «bli», «hverandre» or «seg.»

Some idioms:
Det *spørs* om han kommer. (It is not certain that he'll come.)
Det *kjennes* varmt ut i dag. (It feels hot today.)
Det *høres* bra ut. (That sounds good.)
Vi *sees* snart. (We'll see each other soon.)
De *sloss* seint og tidlig. (They were always fighting.)

PASSIVE
As we have seen, the passive voice can either be expressed through verbs ending in -s or through «bli» followed by the past participle. The -s form has a more limited area of use, for example in legal texts, instructions, recipes and newspaper headlines.
Examples:
Butikkene *stenges* klokken 17. (The shops shut at 5 p.m.)
Dørene *lukkes*. (The doors are closing.)
Fisken *kokes* i 8 minutter. (Poach the fish for 8 minutes.)

In spoken Norwegian «bli» + past participle is more common.
Example:
De fleste avisene *blir skrevet* på bokmål. (Most newspapers are written in «bokmål».)

In general, the passive is used much less frequently in modern Norwegian than the active voice.

Conjugations

All Norwegian verbs can be classified either as regular or irregular.
Examples:
Regular: *lese* (read) – *leste* – *lest*
Irregular: *gå* (go) – *gikk* – *gått*

How to classify a verb:
It is impossible to tell from the verb's appearance in the infinitive
whether it is regular or irregular – conjugations must be learnt for
each individual verb. In most dictionaries all verbs are listed in the
infinitive, with the addition of the past and perfect tenses for the
irregular verbs. In the case of regular verbs only the endings in
the past and perfect tenses are normally included, for example *lese,
-te, -t.*

REGULAR (WEAK) VERBS

	Infinitive	Past	Perfect
a.	å bo (to live)	bodde	bodd
b.	å eie (to own)	eide	eid
c.	å lese (to read)	leste	lest
d.	å vaske (to wash)	vasket	vasket

Knowing that a verb is regular is not enough, as regular verbs have
four possible conjugations. However, some rules do exist, although
there are many exceptions.

a. If the verb ends in a stressed vowel in the infinitive, the past and
   perfect tenses are usually formed by adding *-dde* and *-dd*
   respectively.
   Examples:
   bo (to live) – *bodde* – *bodd*
   sy (to sew) – *sydde* – *sydd*

b. If the verb stem (ie. the infinitive form minus final -e) ends in a
   diphthong, *-g* or *-v,* then *-de* and *-d* are added for the past and
   perfect.

Examples:

pleie (to be accustomed to) – *pleide* – *pleid*
bygge (to build) – *bygde* – *bygd*
leve (to live) – *levde* – *levd*

c. If the verb stem ends in a single consonant, *-te* and *-t* are added.
Examples:
lese (to read) – *leste* – *lest*
høre (to hear) – *hørte* – *hørt*

d. If the verb stem ends in more than one consonant, the past and perfect are usually formed through the addition of *-et* for both tenses.
Examples:
vaske (to wash) – *vasket* – *vasket*
snakke (to talk) – *snakket* – *snakket*

Remember! If you know the past tense form of a regular verb, then you also know the past participle. To form the past participle of a verb which ends in -e in the past tense, simply omit the -e.
Instead of listing more detailed rules with all their exceptions here, we suggest you consult a dictionary when in doubt as to the conjugation of a particular verb.

IRREGULAR VERBS

The most common irregular verbs are listed below. The present tense is only included when its form is irregular. An asterisk indicates that the verb also has a regular form.

Infinitive	Present	Past	Past participle
be (to ask, pray)		bad	bedt
binde (to tie)		bandt	bundet
bite (to bite)		bet	bitt
bli (to stay, become)		ble	blitt
brekke (to break)		brakk	brukket
*brenne (to burn)		brant	brent
bringe (to bring)		brakte	brakt
bryte (to break)		brøt	brutt
by (to offer)		bød	budt
bære (to carry)		bar	båret

41

Infinitive	Present	Past	Past participle
dra (to go, drag)		drog	dratt
drikke (to drink)		drakk	drukket
drive (to drive, operate)		drev	drevet
ete (to eat)		åt	ett
falle (to fall)		falt	falt
finne (to find)		fant	funnet
fly (to fly)		fløy	fløyet
flyte (to float)		fløt	flytt
forlate (to leave)		forlot	forlatt
forsvinne (to disappear)		forsvant	forsvunnet
fortelle (to tell, relate)		fortalte	fortalt
fryse (to freeze)		frøs	frosset
følge (to follow)		fulgte	fulgt
få (to get)		fikk	fått
gi (to give)		gav	gitt
gjelde (to apply)		gjaldt	gjeldt
gjøre (to do)	gjør	gjorde	gjort
gli (to slip)		gled	glidd
gripe (to grasp)		grep	grepet
gråte (to cry)		gråt	grått
gå (to go, walk)		gikk	gått
ha (to have)		hadde	hatt
*henge (to hang)		hang	hengt
hete (to be called)		het	hett
hjelpe (to help)		hjalp	hjulpet
holde (to hold)		holdt	holdt
*klype (to pinch)		kløp	kløpet
knekke (to crack)		knakk	knekket
komme (to come)		kom	kommet
krype (to creep)		krøp	krøpet
kunne (to be able to)	kan	kunne	kunnet
la (to let, allow)		lot	latt
late (to seem)		lot	latt
le (to laugh)		lo	ledd

Infinitive	Present	Past	Past participle
legge (to lay, put)		la	lagt
lide (to suffer)		led	lidd
ligge (to lie)		lå	ligget
*lyde (to sound)		lød	lydt
lyve (to lie)		løy	løyet
løpe (to run)		løp	løpet/løpt
måtte (to have to)	må	måtte	måttet
nyte (to enjoy)		nøt	nytt
*rekke (to reach)		rakk	rukket
*renne (to run)		rant	rent
ri (to ride)		red	ridd
rive (to tear)		rev	revet
ryke (to smoke)		røk	røket
se (to see)		så	sett
selge (to sell)		solgte	solgt
sette (to put, place)		satte	satt
si (to say)	sier	sa	sagt
sitte (to sit)		satt	sittet
skjære (to cut)		skar	skåret
skli (to slide)		skled	sklidd
skrike (to shout)		skrek	skreket
skrive (to write)		skrev	skrevet
skulle (should)	skal	skulle	skullet
skyte (to shoot)		skjøt	skutt
skyve (to push)		skjøv	skjøvet
*slenge (to hang about)		slang	slengt
slippe (to let go)		slapp	sluppet
slite (to pull, tear)		slet	slitt
slå (to hit)		slo	slått
*smelle (to bang)		smalt	smelt
smøre (to spread)		smurte	smurt
sove (to sleep)		sov	sovet
sprekke (to crack)		sprakk	sprukket
springe (to run)		sprang	sprunget
spørre (to ask)	spør	spurte	spurt
stige (to climb)		steg	steget

Infinitive	Present	Past	Past participle
stikke (to sting, pierce)		stakk	stukket
stjele (to steal)		stjal	stjålet
stryke (to iron)		strøk	strøket
stå (to stand)		stod	stått
svi (to sting)		sved	svidd
svike (to betray)		svek	sveket
synge (to sing)		sang	sunget
synke (to sink)		sank	sunket
ta (to take)		tok	tatt
tigge (to beg)		tagg	tigget
tore (to dare)	tør	torde	tort
treffe (to meet)		traff	truffet
trekke (to draw, pull)		trakk	trukket
tvinge (to force)		tvang	tvunget
velge (to choose)		valgte	valgt
ville (to want to)	vil	ville	villet
vinne (to win)		vant	vunnet
vite (to know)	vet	visste	visst
være (to be)	er	var	vært

ARTICLES

Norwegian has two articles, the indefinite and the definite. The articles vary according to the gender of the noun they modify – the complete paradigms are shown below.

The indefinite article in Norwegian functions on the whole the same way as the English indefinite article. The definite article diverges from English on two major counts: a) its position relative to the noun, and b) its form relative to the adjective. These two features often cause initial confusion to the learner of Norwegian, but once the system becomes familiar the rules are in fact very simple:

a. The definite article in Norwegian is *suffixed* to the noun, in striking contrast to most other European languages.

b. When the noun is preceded by an adjective, the suffixed definite article is often retained (see the section on compound and simple definite). However, an additional definite article is compulsory before an adjective, and this form is called the article in relation to adjectives. This usage of the definite article resembles the structure in English.

Example: den store bilen (the big car)

The articles in relation to adjectives have the same form as the demonstrative pronoun (that/those) in Norwegian (see Demonstrative pronouns).

FORM:

Articles in relation to nouns

| | SINGULAR | |
	Indefinite (a)	*Definite* (the)
Masc.	en	-en
Fem.	ei/en	-a
Neut.	et	-et

45

PLURAL

	Indefinite	*Definite* (the)
Masc.		-ene/-ne
Fem.		-ene/-ne
Neut.		-ene/-ne/-a

Examples:

SINGULAR

	Indefinite	*Definite*
Masc.	*en* bil (a car)	bil*en* (the car)
	en lærer	lærer*en* (the teacher)
	(a teacher)	
Fem.	*ei/en* ku (a cow)	ku*a* (the cow)
	ei/en tå (a toe)	tå*a* (the toe)
Neut.	*et* hus (a house)	hus*et* (the house)
	et tre (a tree)	tre*et* (the tree)
	et barn (a child)	barn*et* (the child)

PLURAL

	Indefinite	*Definite*
Masc.	biler (cars)	bil*ene* (the cars)
	lærere (teachers)	lærer*ne* (the teachers)
Fem.	kuer (cows)	ku*ene* (the cows)
	tær (toes)	tær*ne* (the toes)
Neut.	hus (houses)	hus*ene*/hus*a* (the houses)
	trær (trees)	trær*ne* (the trees)
	barn (children)	barn*a* (the children)

Articles in relation to adjectives

These have the same form as the demonstrative pronoun:

Masc.	den	*den* store bilen (the big car)
Fem.	den	*den* store hytta (the big cottage)
Neut.	det	*det* store huset (the big house)
Plural	de	*de* store bilene/hyttene/husene (the big cars/cottages/houses)

Wrong: store bilen, store hytta, store huset.

FUNCTION:

Simple/compound definite
The distinction between the compound definite form and the simple definite form relates to whether the definite article is suffixed to the noun (compound) or not (simple).

SIMPLE DEFINITE
Det hvite hus i Washington (The White House in Washington)
mitt hus (my house)

COMPOUND DEFINITE
det hvite hus*et* der borte (the white house over there)
hus*et mitt* (my house) [the more colloquial usage]

1. **The compound definite form is becoming more and more common in modern Norwegian.**

2. **Simple definite is used:**
   a. **in certain idioms and proper names:**
      Examples:
      Den gamle major (The Old Major – an Oslo restaurant)
      de gode tider (the good times)
      det glade vanvidd (sheer madness)

   b. **in technical expressions and in more formal usage:**
      Examples:
      den kjemiske forbindelse (the chemical compound)
      den rette tro (the true faith)

   c. **in the absolute superlative:**
      Examples:
      uten *den* minste tvil (without the slightest doubt)
      med *de* beste ønsker (with best wishes)

      Note, however, that in direct comparison it is normal to use the compound definite form.

Example:
den eldste sønn*en* (the oldest son)

d. **when the simple noun phrase is supplemented by further information:**
Examples:
Den vietnamesiske pike, Song, bodde her. (The Vietnamese girl Song lived here.)
den vanlige måte å uttrykke seg på (the usual way of expressing oneself)
De studenter som ikke skal ta eksamen, får fri. (The students who are not taking the examination can have the time off.)

In these examples, the compound definite can also be used.

e. **In conjunction with «hele» (all / the whole) and «halve» (half), the definite article in relation to the adjective is dropped:**
Examples:
Han arbeidet *hele dagen.* (He worked all day.)
Wrong: den hele dagen

Hun spiste *hele eplet.* (She ate the whole apple.)
Wrong: det hele eplet

De danset *halve natta.* (They danced half the night.)
Wrong: den halve natta

De leide *halve huset.* (They rented half the house.)
Wrong: det halve huset

Note also the following expressions:
midt på lyse dagen (in broad daylight)
fjerde året på rad (the fourth year in a row)

f. **often in connection with ordinal numbers and «sist» (last), «neste» (next), «forrige» (last, previous), and «samme» (same):**
siste uk*en* / *den* siste uk*en* (the last week)
første dag*en* / *den* første dag*en* (the first day)

forrige onsdag*en* / *den* forrige onsdag*en* (the Wednesday
before / the previous Wednesday)
But note: forrige onsdag (last Wednesday)

The choice here is free between the two alternative definite
forms.

In certain cases the definite article is dropped in these
expressions, for instance when referring to a point of time in
relation to the present.
Examples:
I dag er det 4. november. (Today is the fourth of November.)
En gang i forrige uke var jeg i byen. (Some time last week I
was in town.)
Neste uke skal jeg på ferie. (Next week I'm going on holiday.)
But note:
I fjor var jeg på ferie i Spania. *(Den) første uken* var jeg i
Madrid, og *(den) neste uken* i Segovia. (Last year I was on
holiday in Spain. The first week I was in Madrid and the second
week in Segovia.)

HERE ARE THE GENERAL RULES GOVERNING THE USE OF THE ARTICLES IN MODERN NORWEGIAN

With the indefinite article	Without an article	With the definite article
1. Det var en gang en prins (Once upon a time there was a prince)		
		2. Prinsen het Harald. (The prince was called Harald.)
		3. Mannen på bildet. (The man in the picture.)
		4. Han hentet legen. (He fetched the doctor.)
		5. Løven er dyrenes konge. (The lion is the king of the animals.) Vannet i våre elver . . . (The water in our rivers . . .)
	6. Vann koker ved 100 °C (Water boils at 100 °C)	
	7. Han er lærer. (He is a teacher.)	
Han er en god lærer. (He is a good teacher.)		
8. Han er en luring. (He is a sly one.) Hun er en flink pike. (She's a good girl.)	Det var flink pike! (There's a good girl!)	
	9. Han kjører bil. (He drives a car.)	
	10. Hun skriver med penn. (She writes with a pen.)	
	11. Han tok hatt og frakk. (He took his hat and coat.)	
	12. Rhône, Telemark (the Rhône)	Alpene (The Alps) Nordsjøen (The North Sea)
	13. Maler Hansen (Mr. Hansen the painter)	Themsen (the Thames) Maleren Edv. Munch (The artist Edvard Munch)
	14. Dyktige Liv Ullmann (Talented Liv Ullmann)	Den dyktige Liv Ullmann (The clever Liv Ullmann)

15. i vinter/sommer
(this winter/summer)
til jul/påske/middag
(for Christmas/for Easter/for/to dinner)
på onsdag
(on Wednesday)
i år/dag/morgen/kveld
(this year/today/tomorrow/this evening)
for første og siste gang
(for the first and last time)

om vinteren/sommeren
(in the winter/summer)
til sommeren/vinteren
(next summer/winter)
(midt) på dagen
(in the daytime)
i året
(yearly/a year (as in «once a year»)
i påsken/julen/ ferien
(at Easter/Christmas/in the holidays)

16. i hele dag
(the whole day)

hele dagen
(all day)
halve dagen
(half the day)

samme dag
(the same day)
neste kveld
(the next evening)
siste uke
(the last week)
forrige måned
(last month)
første dag
(the first day)
alle dager
(every day)

samme dagen
(the same day)
neste kvelden
(the next evening)
siste uken
(the last week)
forrige måneden
(the previous month)
første dagen
(the first day)
alle dagene
(all the days)

17. Han tok trikk nummer 2.
(He took the number 2 tram.)
18. min penn / Pers penn
(my pen / Per's pen)
19. hver dag
(each day)
hvilken dag
(which day)

Comments

1.   The indefinite article is used when referring to something which has not yet been mentioned.

2.   The definite article is used when the concept has previously been introduced.

3.   We use the definite article when additional information («på bildet» – in the picture) supplements the noun («mannen» – the man).

4.   The definite article is used in referring to a person or object which is familiar, even if it has not necessarily already been mentioned.

5.   The definite article is used in connection with a particular type or species of animal or object.

6.   The article is omitted in general statements, absolute truths, etc. But when elaborating on the general issue, the definite article is obligatory.

7.   References to profession, occupation, age, nationality and religion omit the article.
Examples:
Som barn var han ofte syk. (As a child he was often ill.)
Hun er katolikk. (She's a Catholic.)
But note:
If an adjective occurs in the description, the article must be retained:
en ivrig katolikk (a dedicated Catholic)
en flink doktor (a good doctor)

8.   The indefinite article is normally used when a description of a person's characteristics is implicit in the noun:
en luring (a sneaky person)

Often the article is dropped in sentences beginning with «Det er/var . . .»
Examples:
Det var god vin! (That was a lovely wine!)
Det var nydelig kjole! (What a lovely dress!)

52

9. In certain set phrases there is no article.

Examples:

ta bil/tog/båt/fly (take the car / the train / the boat / the plane)
å lage mat (to cook)
å bygge hus (to build a house)
å skrive brev (to write a letter)
å dyrke korn (to grow corn)
å legge vin (to make wine)
å spille piano (to play the piano)
å gjøre lykke (to do well)
å kjøpe sko (to buy shoes)
å bake kake (to bake a cake)
å holde selskap (to give a party)
å søke stilling (to apply for a job)

10. The article is not used in various prepositional phrases:

Examples:

å ligge på kne (to kneel)
å hogge med øks (to chop with an axe)
å leve over evne (to live above one's means)
å skjære med kniv (to cut with a knife)
etter avtale (as agreed)
i år (this year)
i dag (today)
i kamp (in battle)
få kornet i hus (bring in the harvest)
å være på vei (to be expecting / to be on the way)
å gå på ski (to go skiing)
fra gammel tid (from the old days)
mot ny innsats (towards a new effort)

11. Set phrases consisting of two coordinated elements omit the article:

pil og bue (bow and arrow)
liv og død (life and death)
hest og kjerre (horse and cart)
skog og mark (woods and fields)
land og strand (up hill and down dale)
liv og lyst (like a dream)
kniv og gaffel (knife and fork)
øks og sag (axe and saw)

12. Geographical names

Some take the definite article, others take no article at all. Each item must be learnt individually.

13. Titles which denote a craft, profession or office, etc. do not include an article:

maler Hansen (Mr. Hansen the painter; i.e. decorator)
snekker Olsen (Mr. Olsen the carpenter)
lærer Johnsen (Mr. Johnsen the teacher)
direktør Jensen (Mr. Jensen the director)
doktor Lie (Mr. Lie the doctor, or: doctor Lie)

The definite article is used in connection with artists, scientists, etc.
Examples:
maler*en* Munch (the artist Munch)
filosof*en* Kant (the philosopher Kant)
sanger*en* Belafonte (the singer Belafonte)
forfatter*en* Tolstoj (the author Tolstoy)

14. In newspaper headlines etc. the article is often left out.

15. Some adverbs of time take the definite article, some don't. See the chapter on these adverbs.

16. With ordinal numbers and «samme», «neste», «siste», «forrige», «alle», use of the definite article varies – see the section on Compound and simple definite forms.

Normally «halve» and «hele» take the definite article:
halve epl*et* (half the apple)
halve bok*a*/banan*en* (half the book / the banana)
hele hus*et*/brød*et*/famili*en*/feri*en*/år*et*/dag*en* (the whole house/loaf/family/holiday/year/day)
But remember:
i hele dag/sommer/vinter/verden (for the whole day/summer/winter; in the whole world)
i hele feri*en*/liv*et*/hus*et*/jul*en*/påsk*en* (for the whole holiday / the whole of one's life / in the whole house / all Christmas / all (of) Easter)

17.   When a noun is followed by a number, the article is not used.
Examples:
Han tok trikken. (He took the tram.)
But:
Han tok trikk nr. 5. (He took tram number 5.)

Passasjerene stod i utgangen. (The passengers stood by the exit.)
But:
De ble bedt om å bruke utgang 3. (They were asked to use exit 3.)

18.   Following the possessive pronoun and the genitive, the article is omitted.

19.   The article is not used following «hver», «hvilken», etc.

NOUNS

Gender

There are three genders in Norwegian:
1. **Masculine**, example: en gutt (a boy)
2. **Feminine**, example: ei jente (a girl)
3. **Neuter**, example: et barn (a child)

How can one tell if a noun is masculine, feminine or neuter?
In general, the form of the noun gives no clue as to its gender, neither are there logical rules. In most cases the gender must be learned for each separate noun. However, here are certain guidelines which may be of help in determining the gender of some nouns, although there are many exceptions.

MASCULINE
1. **Biological gender:** mann (man), gutt (boy), far (father), bror (brother), okse (bull), hane (cockerel).
2. **Plants** (many exceptions): blomst (flower), busk (bush), plante (plant).
3. **Sometimes the noun's ending gives an indication of its gender.**
   -er: hammer (hammer), lærer (teacher), snekker (carpenter), italiener (Italian), tjener (servant), keiser (emperor).
   -ning: bygning (building), skrivning (writing), tenkning (thinking).
   -ing: (can also be feminine): vasking (washing), maling (paint).
   -nad: søknad (application), kostnad (cost), dugnad (communal work).
   -else: hendelse (event), følelse (feeling), forelskelse (love, infatuation).
   But: *et* værelse (room), *et* spøkelse (ghost) – both neuter.
   -het: virkelighet (reality), vanskelighet (difficulty), storhet (greatness).

57

-dom: ungdom (youth), rikdom (wealth), barndom (childhood), lærdom (erudition).
4. **Many loan words.**
(See the following section dealing with which loan words are likely to be neuter. If the noun in question is not to be found there, the likelihood is that its gender is masculine.)

FEMININE

1. **Biological gender:** kone (wife), jente (girl), høne (hen), merr (mare), søster (sister).
2. **Species of trees** (some exceptions): gran (spruce), furu (pine), eik (oak), bjørk (birch).
3. **Nouns ending in -ing can be both masculine and feminine.**
4. **Parts of the body:** nese (nose), hake (chin), hofte (hip), leppe (lip), lever (liver), lunge (lung), tunge (tongue), panne (forehead).
5. **Some nouns which are feminine in dialectal variants of Norwegian are also feminine in «bokmål»:** ku (cow), bikkje (dog), seng (bed), bok (book), klokke (watch), dør (door).
Nouns in the last category can often be difficult for non-native Norwegian speakers to classify, but if in doubt one can safely apply the masculine gender.

NEUTER

1. **Biological gender** (often offspring, many exceptions): barn (child), føll (foal), kje (kid), menneske (person), folk (people).
2. **Names of materials and substances:** jern (iron), stål (steel), sølv (silver), gull (gold), papir (paper), vann (water), gras (grass), høy (hay), korn (corn).
3. **Verbal roots:** skrik (shout), besøk (visit), arbeid (work), rop (call), svar (answer), skriv (letter, note), bad (bath), forsøk (attempt).
Some exceptions, particularly loan words.
4. **Nouns ending in -eri:** maleri (painting), fiskeri (fishery), tyveri (theft), småtteri (trifles, bits and pieces).
5. **Nouns ending in -skap** (many exceptions): selskap (party), ekteskap (marriage), vennskap (friendship), fiendskap (hostility).
But:
en kunnskap (knowledge), *en* lidenskap (passion), *en* egenskap (quality) – all masculine.
6. **Loan words with the following suffixes:**
-al: kvartal (block), arsenal (arsenal).

But:

en festival (festival).

-as: kalas (party).

But:

characterisations of people, e.g. *en* kjekkas (show-off).

-ek: bibliotek (library), diskotek (discoteque).

-em: problem (problem), fonem (phoneme), diadem (diadem).

-tet: universitet (university), fakultet (faculty).

But:

elektrisitet (electricity) and majestet (majesty) – both masculine.

-gram: kilogram (kilogramme), telegram (telegram), program (programme).

-iv: direktiv (directive), initiativ (initiative), motiv (motive).

-ment: departement (department, ministry), arrangement (event, gathering).

-meter: termometer (thermometer), barometer (barometer).

-om: atom (atom), diplom (diploma), idiom (idiom).

-krati: aristokrati (aristocracy), demokrati (democracy).

-um: volum (volume), gymnasium (gymnasium).

Declensions

MASCULINE NOUNS

SINGULAR

Indefinite	*Definite*
1. en gutt (a boy)	gutten (the boy)
2. en mann (a man)	mannen (the man)
3. en ankel (an ankle)	ankelen (the ankle)
4. en tallerken (a plate)	tallerkenen (the plate)
5. en baker (a baker)	bakeren (the baker)
6. en ting (a thing)	tingen (the thing)
7. en modus (a mood)	modusen (the mood)

PLURAL

Indefinite	*Definite*
1. gutter (boys)	guttene (the boys)
2. menn (men)	mennene (the men)
3. ankler (ankles)	anklene (the ankles)
4. tallerkener (plates)	tallerkenene (the plates)

5. bakere (bakers)	bakerne (the bakers)
6. ting (things)	tingene (the things)
7. modi (moods)	modiene (the moods)

Comments:

1. **Illustrates the main rule.**

2. **Vowel change in the plural:**
   A number of nouns (mostly monosyllabic) modify their root vowel in the plural, according to specific patterns:
   Examples:
   a → e: mann (man) – menn, and (duck) – ender, strand (beach) – strender, natt (night) – netter, stang (pole) – stenger, kraft (force) – krefter
   o → ø: fot (foot) – føtter, bonde (farmer) – bønder, bot (fine) – bøter, bok (book) – bøker, rot (root) – røtter
   å → æ: tå (toe) – tær
   å → e: hånd (hand) – hender

   Note also: far (father) – fedre, bror (brother) – brødre

3. **Nouns which end in -el are contracted in the plural and lose the -e. A double consonant is reduced to a single one:**
   en ankel (ankle) – ankler, en apostel (apostle) – apostler, en sykkel (bicycle) – sykler.

4. **Nouns which end in -en keep their full form throughout.**

5. **Nouns ending in -er:**
   The majority drop the final -r of the indefinite plural and the inital e- of the definite plural ending. Some, though, contract in the plural and take -er/-ene, e.g. sommer (summer) – somrer – somrene / vinter (winter) – vintrer – vintrene. Other nouns which behave similarly are finger (finger), åker (field) and alder (age).

   Use the dictionary if in doubt!

6. **Some nouns do not change in the indefinite plural:**
   feil (mistake), kjeks (biscuit), liter (litre), kilo (kilogramme), fot (foot [as a measure of length]), meter (metre), mil (Norwegian mile = 10 kilometres), dollar (dollar), franc (franc), lire (lire), mark

(Deutschmark), pund (pound), ski (ski), kål (cabbage), løk (onion), spiker (nail), sild (herring), laks (salmon), torsk (cod), maur (ant), mygg (mosquito), lus (louse), takk (thanks), kasus (case), sko (shoe), genus (gender), tempus (time).

The last three examples also have inflected plural forms, viz. skor, genera, tempora, but these are only rarely used.

7. **Some loan words have irregular plural forms.**
Examples:
konto (account) – konti, terminus (terminal) – termini.

FEMININE NOUNS

SINGULAR

Indefinite	*Definite*
1. ei jente (a girl)	jenta (the girl)
2. ei aksel (an axle)	aksla (the axle)
3. ei seter (a mountain farm)	setra (the mountain farm)
4. ei frøken (a teacher)	frøkna (the teacher)
5. ei and (a duck)	anda (the duck)
6. ei mus (a mouse)	musa (the mouse)

PLURAL

Indefinite	*Definite*
1. jenter (girls)	jentene (girls)
2. aksler (axles)	akslene (the axles)
3. setrer (mountain farms)	setrene (the mountain farms)
4. frøkner (teachers)	frøknene (the teachers)
5. ender (ducks)	endene (the ducks)
6. mus (mice)	musene (the mice)

Comments:
Some nouns have obligatory feminine gender and these always take -a in the definite singular form.

Examples:
gate (street) – gata (the street)   geit (goat) – geita (the goat)

ku (cow) – kua (the cow)   seng (bed) – senga (the bed)
hytte (cottage) – hytta (the cottage)   fele (fiddle) – fela (the fiddle)

In most cases though, there is a choice between the ending -*a* or -*en* in the definite singular, depending on the dialect or sosiolect of Norwegian being spoken.

1. **Illustrates the main rule.**
2. **Nouns which end in -el are contracted in all forms except the indefinite singular.**
3. **Nouns which end in -er are contracted in all but the basic form. But:**
   ei datter – dattera – døtre(r) – døtrene
   (daughter)
   ei søster – søstera – søstre(r) – søstrene
   (sister)
4. **Nouns which end in -en are contracted in all but the basic form.**
5. **Vowel change in the plural:**
   Examples: and (duck) – ender, bok (book) – bøker.
   Most of these nouns can alternatively take -en in the definite singular – see the section on Masculine nouns, point 2.
   Note: mor (mother) – mødre.
6. **Some nouns remain the same as the basic form,**
   e.g. lus (louse), sild (herring), mil (mile), ski (ski).

NEUTER NOUNS

SINGULAR
Indefinite   *Definite*
1. et år (a year)   året (the year)
2. et eple (an apple)   eplet (the apple)
3. et barn (a child)   barnet (the child)
4. et kjøkken (a kitchen)   kjøkkenet (the kitchen)
5. et teater (a theatre)   { teatret (the theatre)
                                { teateret
6. et tempel (a temple)   { templet (the temple)
                                { tempelet
7. et sted (a place)   stedet (the place)
8. et håndkle (a towel)   håndkleet (the towel)
9. et museum (a museum)   museet (the museum)

PLURAL

Indefinite	*Definite*
1. år (years)	årene/åra (the years)
2. epler (apples)	eplene (the apples)
3. barn (children)	barna (the children)
4. kjøkken/kjøkkener (kitchens)	kjøkkenene (the kitchens)
5. teater/teatre (theatres)	teatrene (the theatres)
6. templer (temples)	templene (the temples)
7. steder (places)	stedene (the places)
8. håndklær (towels)	håndklærne (the towels)
9. museer (museums)	museene (the museums)

Comments:

1. **The majority of monosyllabic neuter nouns behave in this way.** Certain polysyllabic nouns follow the same pattern, in particular compound nouns: e.g. eventyr (adventure), poeng (point), tiltak (venture), forhold (relationship), anlegg (works), unntak (exception), spørsmål (question), etc.
2. **This pattern holds for most neuter nouns ending in unstressed -e.**
3. **Some nouns always take the ending -a in the definite plural form:** bein (leg), garn (wool), dyr (animal), troll (troll), krøtter (cattle), kje (kid).
4. **Nouns which end in -en behave as the example given,** with the exception of våpen (weapon) – våpenet – våpen – våpnene.
5. **Exceptions to the general rule for nouns ending in -er:** et krydder (spice) – krydderet – krydder – krydderne et sukker (sugar) – sukkeret et lager (store) – lageret – lager/lagre – lagrene.
6. **Nouns ending in -el all contract for the plural, while contraction is optional in the definite singular.**
7. **Some monosyllabic neuter nouns take -er in the indefinite plural:** lem (limb), felt (field), punkt (point), stoff (material), tøy (clothing), skrift (publication), blad (magazine).
8. **Vowel change in the plural:** kne (knee) – knær, forkle (apron) – forklær, håndkle (towel) – håndklær, tre (tree) – trær.
9. **Many loan words have special inflected forms – use the dictionary!**

More about the singular and plural

1. **Some nouns are used only in the singular:**
   a. **Names of substances:** jern (iron), vann (water), øl (beer), gull (gold).
      But: Jeg vil ha tre øl. (I want three beers.)
   b. **Abstract nouns:** visdom (wisdom), lykke (happiness), godhet (goodness), skjønnhet (beauty).
      But: skjønnheter (beautiful people)
   c. **Class nouns:** mat (food), drikke (drink), løv (foliage), frukt (fruit), papir (paper).
      But: «frukt» and «papir» can also take the plural forms when referring to individual items of the class.

2. **Some nouns when used in the singular denote a general class as opposed to individual items:**
   Examples:
   koke *fisk* (to cook fish)
   De fant mye *sopp*. (They found a lot of mushrooms.)
   Det er mye *elg* i skogen. (There is a lot of elk in the forest.)
   But: Han fikk ti *fisker* på kroken. (He hooked 10 fish.)
   De skjøt to *elger*. (They shot two elks.)

3. **Some nouns are normally only used in the plural:**
   a. **People:** foreldre (parents), søsken (siblings), forfedre (ancestors).

   b. **Animals:** høns (poultry).

   c. **Things:** briller (glasses), grønnsaker (vegetables), penger (money), klær (clothes), bukser (trousers).
      These can occasionally also be used in the singular.

Definite or indefinite form

1. **See the chapters on Articles and Pronouns.**

2. **The indefinite form of the noun is always used in the following constructions:**
   a. *Hver* dag (Every day)
      Hvert år (Every year)

b. *Hvilken* dag? (Which day?)
   Hvilket år? (Which year?)
   Hvilke bøker? (Which books?)
   Hva slags bok/bøker? (What sort of book(s)?)
c. *Noen* dager (Some days)
   Ikke noen dager ⎱ (Not any days)
   Ingen dager ⎰
   Ingen dag ⎱ (Not any day)
   Ikke noen dag ⎰
   Noe vann (Some water)
   Ikke noe vann (Not any water)
d. *Flere* dager (Several days)
   Mange dager (Many days)
   To dager (Two days)
   But:
   De to dag*ene* . . . (The/those two days . . .)
   Mye mat (A lot of food)
e. *Neste* dag/time/måned . . . (next day/hour/month . . .)
   Forrige uke/måned . . . (last week/month . . .)
   Siste time(n), uke(n), måned(en) (the last hour, week, month)
   I *hele* dag (the whole day)
   But: hele dag*en* (all day)
   for første gang (for the first time)
f. *min* stol (my chair), **but:** stol*en* min
   Pers stol (Per's chair), **but:** stol*en* til Per.

Case

Only two nominal cases are in use in modern Norwegian: the *nominative* and the *genitive*.

NOMINATIVE:
Example: gutt (boy) – gutten (the boy) – gutter (boys) – guttene (the boys)

GENITIVE:
Example: gutts (boy's) – guttens (the boy's) – gutters (boys') – guttenes (the boys')

1. a. The genitive case is formed by adding the ending -s to the nominative form.
   b. Some proper nouns have a special form in the genitive:
      Jes*u* liv (the life of Jesus)
      Krist*i* fødsel (the birth of Christ)
   c. If the nominative form already ends in -s, the genitive is represented by an apostrophe:
      Jens' hatt (Jens' hat)
      Moss' innbyggere (the inhabitants of the town of Moss)
   d. The group genitive: the -s suffix is added to the last element only of a noun phrase:
      mor og far*s* eneste barn (mother and father's only child)

2. **The genitive following the preposition «til»:**
   In certain idioms «til» is followed by a noun in the genitive:
   til sjøs (to sea), til sengs (to bed), til fots (on foot), til fjells (to the mountains), til havs (to (the) sea), til værs (up in the air), til bords (to the table).

3. **Note the use of the genitive in the following expressions:**
   tre mils vei (a road that is three Norwegian miles long)
   to kroners frimerke (a stamp costing two kroner)
   en times tid (approx. one hour's time)

4. **The genitive is used less and less frequently in modern spoken Norwegian, giving way instead to expressions incorporating a preposition.**
   Example: guttens bil → bilen til gutten (the boy's car)

   The preposition can vary:
   Examples:
   skogens blomster → blomstene *i* skogen (the flowers in the forest)
   prestens datter → datteren *til* presten (the priest's daughter)
   gårdens folk → folka *på* gården (the farm people)
   husets datter → dattera *i* huset (the daughter of the house)
   kjolens pris → prisen *på* kjolen (the price of the dress)
   Norges konge → kongen *i* Norge (Norway's king / the king of Norway)

Often the genitive form is reserved for rather more formal use, while expressions containing a preposition are more typical of everyday speech.

In certain idioms the genitive form is compulsory:
Examples:

dagens slit (the daily toil)   en times tid (an hour's time)
verdens ende (the end of the world) nattens søvn (the night's sleep)
livets gang (the passage of life)   sorgens time (the hour of grief)

DATIVE
Examples:

på tide: Nå er det *på tide* at du kommer. (Now it's about time that you came.)
i live: Vi håper at alle i båten er *i live*. (We hope everyone in the boat is alive.)
av gårde: De dro *av gårde* i hui og hast. (They left in a hurry.)

The dative case occurs only in a few fossilized idioms.

Compound nouns

NOUN + NOUN
In compound nouns the last element determines the gender of the word.
Examples:
en bilrute (a car window), et bildekk (a car tyre).

1. **Simple compounding** – the most common form:
   tekopp (teacup), bokhylle (bookshelf).

2. **Compounding with -s-:**
   The following rules offer some guidelines for forming compound nouns with a linking -s-:

   a. **The first element is in the genitive case,** e.g.
      morsmål (mother tongue), dagsreise (day's journey).

   b. **The first element is a loan word ending in -ion, -sjon, -tet or -ment,** e.g.
      religionshistorie (history of religion), stasjonsmester (station master), universitetsbygning (university building), departementsråd (permanent secretary (Government)).

c. **In most cases where the first element ends in -dom, -else, -het, -ing, -ning or -skap,** e.g.
barndomsbilde (childhood portrait), utdannelsespolitikk (educational policy), storhetstid (period of greatness), kjærlighetsdrap (crime of passion), kringkastingshus (broadcasting house).

Exceptions:
- where the first element denotes a person or group of people ending in -ing, e.g. vikingtid (Viking age)
- English loan words ending in -ing, e.g. campingvogn (caravan)
- certain words ending in -ing which are not derived from a verb, e.g. honningkrukke (honey jar)

d. **The first element ends in -sel:**
fengselsport (prison gate), ferdselsåre (traffic artery).

e. **The first element ends in -nad, -et or -ed:**
søknadsfrist (deadline for applications), levnetsløp (career), månedslønn (monthly salary)

f. **When the first element is itself composed of a compound noun, a linking -s- is often inserted between the first and second element,** e.g.
saueskinn*s*kåpe (sheepskin coat), varmtvann*s*kran (hot water tap)
But: skinnkåpe (fur coat), vannkran (water tap)

3. **Compounding with -e-:**
Linking -e- occurs usually when the first element refers to animals, plants or people, e.g.
barnebarn (grandchild), vennekrets (circle of friends), sauekjøtt (mutton (literally: sheep meat)), erteblomst (sweet pea).

Other examples include:
bygdemål (rural dialect), julekveld (Christmas night)

ADJECTIVE + NOUN
a. **The adjective is normally uninflected:**
grovbrød (brown bread)   snarvei (shortcut)

penklær (party clothes)   storfolk (VIPs)
godvær (fair weather)   hvitvask (whites (washing clothes))

b. **There are a few exceptions to this general rule:**
varmtvann (hot water)   kaldtvann (cold water)
godtfolk (gentlefolk)

VERB + NOUN
reiseselskap (travel agency)   skrivebok (exercise book)
spisevaner (eating habits)   svømmevest (life jacket)
sovevogn (sleeping car)   løpebane (racetrack)

PREPOSITION + NOUN
opprop (roll call)   overtro (superstition)
omtanke (consideration)   underverden (underworld)
ettersyn (inspection)   baktanke (ulterior motive)

ADVERB + NOUN
hjemmehjelp (home help)   frammøte (attendance)
bortekamp (away match)   nærkontakt (close contact)
uteklær (outdoor clothes)   midtbane (mid-field)

ADJECTIVES

In Norwegian, the adjective always agrees in number and gender with the noun. The plural form of the adjective is the same for all genders. The adjective also has two declensions: the indefinite (exemplified by «en stor bil» (a big car)), and the definite (as in «den store bilen» (the big car)).

Declensions

REGULAR DECLENSION

SINGULAR

	Indefinite	*Definite*
Masc.	en *stor* bil (a big car)	den *store* bilen (the big car)
Fem.	ei *stor* hytte (a big cottage)	den *store* hytta (the big cottage)
Neut.	et *stort* hus (a big house)	det *store* huset (the big house)

PLURAL

	Indefinite	*Definite*
Masc.	*store* biler (big cars)	de *store* bilene (the big cars)
Fem.	*store* hytter (big cottages)	de *store* hyttene (the big cottages)
Neut.	*store* hus (big houses)	de *store* husene (the big houses)

Note also that the adjective declines in the same way when placed predicatively:
Bilen er *stor*. (The car is big.)
Hytta er *stor*. (The cottage is big.)
Huset er *stort*. (The house is big.)
Bilene er *store*. (The cars are big.)
Hyttene er *store*. (The cottages are big.)
Husene er *store*. (The houses are big.)

The majority of adjectives are declined in the same way as «stor.» There are only three different forms:
«stor» is used only in the indefinite masculine and feminine singular;
«stort» is used only in the indefinite neuter singular;
«store» is used in all the other forms.

IRREGULAR FORMS

Irregular spelling

dum, dumt, dumme (silly)
Most adjectives ending in -m double the final consonant before -e.

trygg, trygt, trygge (safe)
A double consonant is reduced to a single one before -t.
(Exceptions: fullt (full), visst (certain), spisst (sharp))

gammel, gammelt, gamle (old)
vakker, vakkert, vakre (pretty)
åpen, åpent, åpne (open)
Adjectives ending in -el, -er and -en lose the -e when the -e of the adjectival inflection is added. A double consonant will at the same time be reduced to a single.

ny, nytt, nye (new)
Adjectives ending in a stressed vowel usually take a double -t in the neuter singular, though there are some exceptions:
bra (good), tro (faithful), sky (shy), sjalu (jealous), kry (proud).
These adjectives take no inflection at all throughout the declension. There are also examples of polysyllabic adjectives ending in a vowel which do not inflect; edru (sober) and lilla (lilac) are illustrations of this last point.

grei, greit, greie (easy)
Only a single -t is added in the neuter form to adjectives ending in a diphthong.

The following adjectives do not inflect for number or gender

a. **Certain adjectives which end in a stressed vowel:**

bra (good)	sta (stubborn)	kry (proud)
tro (faithful)	ru (rough)	edru (sober)
sky (shy)	slu (sly)	lilla (lilac)
sjalu (jealous)		

Examples:
den *edru* mannen (the sober man)
et *bra* bilde (a good picture)
eslene er *sta* (the mules are stubborn)

b. **Adjectives which end in an unstressed -e:**

øde (deserted)	sovende (sleeping)	bedre (better)
stille (quiet)	syngende (singing)	penere (prettier)
steinete (stony)	gående (walking)	mindre (smaller)

Examples:
et *øde* område (a deserted area)
et *sovende* barn (a sleeping child)
mannen var *stille* (the man was quiet)

c. **Some adjectives ending in -s:**

stakkars (poor)	gratis (free)	nymotens (newfangled)
avsides (remote)	felles (mutual)	forgjeves (in vain)
avleggs (out of date)	delvis (partly)	innvortes (internal)

Examples:
stakkars mennesker! (poor people!)
et *gratis* måltid (a free meal)
klærne er *avleggs* (the clothes are out of date)

The following adjectives do not take -t in the neuter form, but are otherwise regular

a. **Adjectives ending in -(l)ig:**

heldig (lucky)	vennlig (friendly)	vanskelig (difficult)
lykkelig (happy)	yndig (graceful)	forsiktig (careful)

Examples:
et *lykkelig* minne (a happy memory)
   But: *lykkelige* minner (happy memories)
et *vennlig* smil (a friendly smile)
   But: det *vennlige* smilet (the friendly smile)

b. **Some adjectives which already end in -t – in particular loan words, superlatives and participles:**

svart/sort (black)	moderat (moderate)	flott (smart)
kort (short)	skrevet (written)	lat (lazy)
interessant (interesting)	størst (biggest)	kåt (wanton)

Examples:
et *svart* skjørt (a black skirt)
   But: det *svarte* skjørtet (the black skirt)
et *lat* individ (a lazy individual)
   But: det *late* individet (the lazy individual)

Certain other adjectives take an extra -t in the neuter form:
et *hvitt* hus (a white house)
   But: det *hvite* huset (the white house)
et *søtt* ansikt (a sweet face)
   But: det *søte* ansiktet (the sweet face)

c. **Adjectives ending in -sk which denote nationality or which are polysyllabic:**

norsk (Norwegian)	krigersk (warlike)	fantastisk (fantastic)
engelsk (English)	historisk (historical)	praktisk (practical)
indisk (Indian)	rebelsk (rebellious)	mekanisk (mechanical)

Examples:
et *norsk* frimerke (a Norwegian stamp)
   But: det *norske* frimerket (the Norwegian stamp)
et *fantastisk* bilde (a fantastic picture)
   But: det *fantastiske* bildet (the fantastic picture)

However, note that monosyllabic adjectives ending in -sk decline regularly.
Examples:
et *ferskt* brød (a fresh loaf)
et *friskt* barn (a healthy child)

d. Some adjectives ending in -d:

solid (solid)	utlevd (decrepit)	fremmed (foreign)
stupid (stupid)	absurd (absurd)	lærd (learned)
redd (afraid)	glad (happy)	

Examples:

et *solid* hus (a solid house)
   But: det *solide* huset (the solid house)
et *absurd* svar (an absurd reply)
   But: det *absurde* svaret (the absurd reply)

Normally, adjectives ending in -d add a -t in the neuter:
et *rødt* hus (a red house)
et *bredt* belte (a broad belt)

The following adjectives take double -t in the neuter and omit the final -e in the other forms

blå, blått, blå (blue)
grå, grått, grå (grey)
rå, rått, rå (raw)
skrå, skrått, skrå (slanting)

Examples:
et *blått* hav (a blue ocean)
det *blå* havet (the blue ocean)
mange *blå* hav (many blue oceans)

The entire declension of the adjective «liten» is irregular

Masculine:
en *liten* gutt (a small boy)
den *lille* gutten (the small boy)
små gutter (small boys)
de *små* guttene (the small boys)

Feminine:
ei *lita* jente (a small girl)
den *lille* jenta (the small girl)
små jenter (small girls)
de *små* jentene (the small girls)

Neuter:
et *lite* barn (a small child)
det *lille* barnet (the small child)
små barn (small children)
de *små* barna (the small children)

Remember that the plural form «små» (small) does not take -e.

Litt (a little) – lite (little):
Han snakker *litt* norsk. (He speaks a little Norwegian.)
Han snakker *lite* norsk. (He speaks little Norwegian.)
Hun spiser svært *lite*. (She eats very little.)
Hun spiser *litt* mat nå. (She eats a little food now.)

Note that «veldig» and «svært» (both mean «very») cannot be used with «litt»:

Wrong: Hun spiser veldig litt mat.

Idiomatic use:
Det var *litt av en* fisk! (That was quite a fish!)

«ANNEN», «ANNET», «ANDRE» (OTHER, DIFFERENT)

1. en *annen* vei (another way)
   den *andre* veien (the other way)
   et *annet* hus (another house, a different house)
   det *andre* huset (the other house)
   andre veier/hus (other ways/houses)
   de *andre* veiene/husene (the other ways/houses)

   Wrong: en andre vei, et andre hus

2. **Note the use of «annen», «andre» in the following expressions to mean «second»:**
   Den *annen/andre* mai (the second of May)
   Dronning Elisabeth den *annen/andre* (Queen Elizabeth the second)
   Jeg går i *annen/andre* klasse. (I'm in the second year at school.)
   Jeg bor i *annen/andre* etasje. (I live on the second floor.)

75

In these and similar examples, there is no difference between «annen» and «andre». However, note that «den andre dagen» means «the second day»; «the other day» would normally be rendered by an expression such as «forleden dag»:
Jeg så Per forleden dag. (I saw Per the other day.)

As «den/det andre» can mean both «the other» and «the second», ambiguities can arise in certain cases.
For example:
«De bor i det andre huset.» can mean:
1) they live in the second house (as opposed to the first in the street)
2) they live in the other house (as opposed to the one we were looking at).
Normally, context and, in spoken Norwegian, stress and intonation patterns will reduce the possibilities of confusion.

Note also the difference between:
på den *annen* side (on the other hand; ie. an abstraction)
and
på den *andre* siden (on the other side; ie. literal meaning)

«Every other» is expressed by «annenhver»:
Han går på skolen *annenhver* dag. (He goes to school every other day.)
De møtes *annethvert* år. (They meet every other year.)

Note that both parts of the adjective decline according to the gender of the noun following.

«Egen» (own) also has irregularities in its declensions:
min *egen* dør (my own door)
   But: min *åpne* dør (my open door)
mitt *eget* vindu (my own window)
   But: mitt *åpne* vindu (my open window)
mine *egne* dører/vinduer (my own doors/windows)
   But: mine *åpne* dører/vinduer (my open doors/windows)

Wrong: min egne dør, mitt egne hus

«MANGE» AND «MYE»

«Mange» (many, a lot of) is used with count nouns in the plural:
Examples:
mange bøker (many (or: a lot of) books)
mange ønsker (many wishes)
mange elever (many pupils)
mange epler (many apples)
mange penger (a lot of money), or: mye penger
mange rom (many rooms)

«Mye» (much, a lot of) is used with mass nouns:
Examples:
mye olje (a lot of oil)
mye frukt (a lot of fruit)
mye luft (a lot of air)
mye tid (a lot of time)
mye penger (a lot of money), or: mange penger
mye smør (a lot of butter)

THE INDEFINITE FORM OF THE ADJECTIVE

An adjective appears in the indefinite form:
1. **when it is not preceded by a determiner:**
   stor bil (big car), *grønt* gras (green grass).
2. **after the indefinite article:**
   en *stor* bil (a big car)
3. **after numerals:**
   ett *stort* hus (one big house)
4. **after «ikke noen/ingen» and «ikke noe»:**
   ikke noen/ingen *stor* bil (not a big car)
   ikke noe *stort* hus (not a big house)
5. **after «hver, hvert»:**
   hver *stor* bil (each big car)
   hvert *stort* hus (each big house)
   and «enhver, ethvert»:
   enhver *stor* bil (every big car)
   ethvert *stort* hus (every big house)
6. **after «noe»:**
   noe *godt* øl (some good beer)

77

7. **after «hvilken/hvilket»:**
   hvilken *fin* bil (what a fine car)
   hvilket *fint* hus (what a fine house)
8. **after «all, alt»:**
   all *ny* snø (all new snow)
   alt *nytt* stoff (all new material)
9. **when the adjective is predicative:**
   Bilen er *stor*. (The car is big.)
   Huset er *stort*. (The house is big.)
   Du ser *dum* ut. (You look silly.)
   Hun fant huset *tomt*. (She found the house empty.)

THE DEFINITE FORM OF THE ADJECTIVE

The adjective appears in the definite form:
1. **after the definite article:**
   den *fine* bilen (the fine car)
2. **after the demonstrative pronouns:**
   den/denne *fine* bilen (that/this fine car)
3. **after the possessive pronoun:**
   min *lille* venn (my little friend)
   mitt *store* eple (my large apple)
   Note: The exception to this rule is
     mitt *eget* hus (my own house)
     min *egen* bil (my own car), etc. See «Egen».
4. **after the personal pronoun in exclamations:**
   Jeg *arme* mann! (poor me!)
   Du *store* min! (good heavens!)
5. **after the genitive -s:**
   Pers *nye* hatt (Per's new hat)
   hærens *store* tap (the army's great loss)
6. **in some cases before a noun without a preceding article, usually when the adjective forms part of a proper name, and in expressions of address:**
   gamle Norge (old Norway), lille venn (little friend), kjære barn (dear child)
7. **in certain prepositional phrases:**
   i hele dag (the whole day)
   midt på lyse dagen (in broad daylight)
   ut av løse luften (out of thin air)

med største fornøyelse (with the greatest of pleasure)
i verste fall (if the worst comes to the worst)
8. **after «første, siste, neste, samme» (first, last, next, same):**
neste *offentlige* møte (the next public meeting)

Remember the correct form of the adjective after the definite article and other determiners is always -e (except for the adjectives which never take -e!).

SUCCESSIVE ADJECTIVES

«Et lite pent ansikt» can mean either:
1. a not very pretty face, or
2. a small, pretty face,
whereas «et pent lite ansikt» can only mean: a pretty, small face.

When more than one adjective precedes the noun, the least «objective» of them usually comes first:
en hyggelig, gammel kvinne (a pleasant old woman)
en enfoldig, ung mann (a simple young man)

THE PAST PARTICIPLE USED AS AN ADJECTIVE

Some past participles ending in -et can be used adjectivally. Where two alternatives are given, both are equally acceptable.
a. **Participles of strong verbs:**
en *stjålet/stjålen* bil (a stolen car)
den *stjålne* bilen (the stolen car)
de *stjålne* bilene (the stolen cars)

et *stjålet* skip (a stolen ship)
det *stjålne* skipet (the stolen ship)
de *stjålne* skipene (the stolen ships)

b. **Participles of weak verbs:**
en *vasket* kopp (a washed cup)
den *vaskede/vaskete* koppen (the washed cup)
et *vasket* gulv (a washed floor)
det *vaskede/vaskete* gulvet (the washed floor)

79

The plural form of the adjective is the same as the definite singular.

Note that when the adjective is in the predicative position, the participles will normally have the same form as the indefinite singular:
Bilen er *stjålet*. (The car is stolen.)
Skipet er *stjålet*. (The ship is stolen.)
Bilene er *stjålet*. (The cars are stolen.)

c. **The participles of some strong verbs resemble «åpen» in their declension (see page 71) and behave like regular adjectives:**
velkommen (welcome), løssluppen (unbridled), veloppdragen (well brought-up), kjærkommen (welcome), vrien (difficult, awkward).
Example:
et kjærkommen*t* brev (a welcome letter)

OTHER ADJECTIVES ENDING IN -ET

a. **Adjectives which are not derived from verbs:**
hullet(e) (full of holes), fillet(e) (ragged), steinet(e) (stony), etc.
Examples:
en *steinet/steinete* vei (a stony road)
den *steinete* veien (the stony road)
(This type of adjective cannot take the alternative ending -ede.)

b. **Compound adjectives:**
langermet (long-sleeved), trekantet (triangular)
Examples:
en *langermet* genser (a long-sleeved sweater)
den *langermede/-ete* genseren (the long-sleeved sweater)

COMPARISON OF ADJECTIVES

A **The majority of adjectives have an absolute, a comparative and a superlative form as exemplified by:**

Absolute	*Comparative*	*Superlative*
trygg (safe)	trygg*ere* (safer)	trygg*est* (safest)

B Exceptions:

1. **Adjectives ending in -er, -el and -en contract in the comparative and superlative:**
   Examples:

mager (thin)	ma*gr*ere	ma*gr*est
simpel (simple)	sim*pl*ere	sim*pl*est
moden (ripe)	mo*dn*ere	mo*dn*est

2. **Adjectives ending in -(l)ig and -som take -st and not -est in the superlative:**
   Examples:

nyttig (useful)	nyttigere	nyttig*st*
vanskelig (difficult)	vanskeligere	vanskelig*st*
morsom (amusing)	morsommere	morsom*st*

Note that the final -m of -som is doubled before the vowel in the comparative.

3. **Many adjectives have irregular forms in the comparative and superlative. A number of adjectives, marked *, lack a positive form, and have only a comparative and superlative form. The missing positive form must be replaced by an adverb to complete the paradigm.**

bra/god (good)	bedre	best
dårlig/ille (bad) ond/vond	} verre	verst
få (few)	færre	færrest
gammel (old)	eldre	eldst
lang (long)	lengre	lengst
liten (small)	mindre	minst
mange (many)	flere	flest
mye (much)	mer	mest
nær (near)	{ nærmere	nærmest
	(nærere	nærest: in the abstract sense)
stor (large)	større	størst
tung (heavy)	tyngre	tyngst
ung (young)	yngre	yngst
*bak (behind)	bakre (rear)	bakerst (rearmost)
*borte (away)	bortre (farther)	bortest (farthest)

81

*fremme (in front)	fremre («anterior»)	fremst ⎫ (foremost)
*foran (in front of)		forrest ⎭
*inne (inside)	indre (inner)	innerst (innermost)
*midt (middle)	midtre (centre)	midterst (centremost)
*nede (down)	nedre (lower)	nederst (lowest)
*nord (north)	nordre (northern)	nordligst (northernmost)
*oppe (up)	øvre (upper)	øverst (uppermost)
*sør (south)	søndre (southern)	sørligst (southernmost)
*vest (west)	vestre (western)	vestligst (westernmost)
*øst (east)	østre (eastern)	østligst (easternmost)
*ute (out)	ytre (outer)	ytterst (utmost)
*under (under)		underst (bottommost)

*denotes adverbs.

4. **Periphrastic forms of comparison where the use of «mer, mest» (more, most) is obligatory:**
   a. **Participles**

elsket (loved)	mer elsket (more loved)	mest elsket (most loved)
slitt (worn out)	mer slitt	mest slitt
vinnende (winning)	mer vinnende	mest vinnende
bebodd (inhabited)	mer bebodd	mest bebodd

   b. **Adjectives ending in -et(e) and -ed:**

steinet(e) (stony)	mer steinet(e)	mest steinet(e)
fillet(e) (ragged)	mer fillet(e)	mest fillet(e)
fremmed (alien)	mer fremmed	mest fremmed

   c. **Polysyllabic adjectives ending in -sk:**

krigersk (warlike)	mer krigersk	mest krigersk
sympatisk (likeable)	mer sympatisk	mest sympatisk

Note that the adjective «norsk» (Norwegian) has two alternatives in the comparative and superlative:
mer norsk/norskere – mest norsk/norskest

d. **Indeclinable adjectives ending in -s:**

avsides (remote)	mer avsides	mest avsides
avleggs (out of date)	mer avleggs	mest avleggs

e. **Compound adjectives:**

selvsikker (self-confident)	mer selvsikker	mest selvsikker
fordelaktig (advantageous)	mer fordelaktig	mest fordelaktig

f. **Other polysyllabic adjectives:**

interessant (interesting)	mer interessant	mest interessant
komplisert (complicated)	mer komplisert	mest komplisert

C Best/beste

Examples:

Hun kan både matematikk, historie og geografi, men hun er *best* i fysikk. (She is good at mathematics, history and geography, but she is best at physics.)

Hun er faktisk den *beste* i klassen. (She is in fact best in the class.)

The indefinite form is used when she is being compared with herself, while the definite form is used in comparison with others.

D Absolute comparative and superlative

Sometimes the comparative and superlative can be used to express a certain degree of a particular attribute without implying direct comparison. Often the English adjectival suffix «-ish» conveys a similar meaning to the Norwegian absolute comparative.

Examples:

Jeg traff en *eldre* herre i byen. (I met an elderly man in town.)

Han har vært her i *lengre* tid. (He has been here for quite a long time.)

De har en *større* eiendom rett utenfor byen. (They have a biggish property on the outskirts of town.)

Vi spiste en *bedre* middag. (We ate quite a good dinner.)

Du må betale et *mindre* gebyr. (You must pay a smallish fee.)

Det er ikke det *minste* rart. (It's not the least strange.)

De lever i den *dypeste* fattigdom. (They live in extreme poverty.)
Det går de *utroligste* rykter. (There are some incredible rumours about.)
Vil du gjøre det? Ja, med *største* fornøyelse. (Will you do it? Yes, with the greatest of pleasure.)

CONCORD

1. **An adjective placed predicatively agrees with the noun it refers to in number and gender:**
Huset er *tomt*. (The house is empty.)
Husene er *tomme*. (The houses are empty.)
Jeg fant husene *tomme*. (I found the houses empty.)

Note: Jeg er *dum*. (I am silly.)
   Jeg føler meg *dum*. (I feel silly.)
   Jeg ser *dum* ut. (I look silly.)

Exceptions:
a. **When the adjective is part of a set phrase, the plural inflection is often dropped:**
   de var glad i hverandre (they loved each other)
   vi er oppmerksom på (we are aware of)
   vi vil være takknemlig for (we will be grateful for)
   jeg slapp hundene løs (I let the dogs go)
   holde pengene klar (have your money ready)
   de var gift (they were married)
   å være klar over (to realize)
   å være lei for (to be sorry about)
   å være vant til (to be used to)
   etc.

b. **Many expressions involving the use of the reflexive pronoun:**
   å drikke seg full (to get drunk)
   å gå seg vill (to get lost)
   å spise seg mett (to eat one's fill)
   å holde seg rolig (to keep still),
   etc.

In the majority of expressions like these the adjective remains uninflected; however, there are some less clear cases. Note the distinction between the following two examples:

Vi er *glad* i dette landet. (We love this country.)

Vi er *glade* i dette landet. (We are happy in this country.)

c. **Doubt can arise when grammatical number and gender conflict with reality.**

Det nygifte paret så *lykkelig(e)* ut. (The newly wed couple looked happy.)

Grammatically, the adjective here should be in the singular, but the plural form seems more natural in the context of two people.

d. **When the rules of concord do not apply:**

When stating generalities, the adjective usually appears in the neuter singular, regardless of the noun's number and gender.

Examples:

Roser er *pent*. (Roses are pretty.)

Sigaretter er *skadelig*. (Cigarettes are harmful.)

Frukt og grønnsaker er *dyrt*. (Fruit and vegetables are expensive.)

Mat er *godt*. (Food is nice.)

Note that in the case of living beings the main rules of concord normally apply:

Elefanter er *store*. (Elephants are big.)

2. **Where there is a string of two or more coordinate subjects, the adjective is usually in the plural:**

Eva og Kari er *friske*. (Eva and Kari are well.)

Både Eva og Kari er *friske*. (Both Eva and Kari are well.)

Såvel Eva som Kari er *friske*. (Both Eva and Kari alike are well.)

Verken Eva eller Kari er *friske*. (Neither Eva nor Kari is well.)

Note especially the last of these four examples, where Norwegian uses a plural form for a construction which in English takes the singular.

Exceptions:

a. **See 1,d. above.**

b. **When the coordinate subjects do not refer to living beings, the principle of proximity applies, ie. the adjective agrees with the noun closest to it:**
Verken pennen eller papiret var *godt*. (Neither the pen nor the paper was good.)
Stolene og bordet var *nytt*. (The chairs and the table were new.)

c. **The same principle applies to coordination with «eller» (or), «enten – eller» (either – or) and «ikke bare – men også» (not only – but also):**
Vinduet eller døra er *åpen*. (The window or the door is open.)
Enten eplet eller pæren er *moden*. (Either the apple or the pear is ripe.)
Ikke bare moren, men også barna var *syke*. (Not only the mother but also the children were ill.)
Ikke bare barna, men også moren var *syk*. (Not only the children but also the mother was ill.)

ADVERBS

MANY ADVERBS ARE DERIVED FROM THE CORRESPONDING ADJECTIVE

Adjective		*Adverb*
pen (pretty)	→	pent (prettily)
Hun er *pen*.		Hun synger *pent*.
(She is pretty.)		(She sings prettily.)
god (good)	→	godt (good/well)
god mat		Maten smakte *godt*.
(good food)		(The food tasted good.)
lang (long)	→	langt (a long way, far)
Veien er *lang*.		De kjørte *langt*.
(The road is long.)		(They drove a long way.)

These and similar adverbs are identical to the neuter form of the adjective.

Adjectives which do not take -t in the indefinite neuter singular also omit the -t in the adverbial form:

bra (good)	→	bra (well)
et *bra* instrument		Hun sang *bra*.
(a good instrument)		(She sang well.)
hyggelig (pleasant)	→	hyggelig (pleasantly)
et *hyggelig* brev		Han pratet *hyggelig*.
(a pleasant letter)		(He chatted pleasantly.)

moderne (modern)	→	moderne (modernly)
et *moderne* hus		Han kledde seg *moderne*.
(a modern house)		(He dressed modernly.)

MANY ADVERBS ARE NOT DERIVED FROM OTHER PARTS OF SPEECH

fram (forward)	jo (indeed)	ut (out)
her (here)	aldri (never)	ellers (otherwise)
der (there)	slik (such)	ned (down)
nok (probably)	hvor (where)	bort (away)

SOME ADVERBS ARE COMPOUNDS

alltid (always)	ingensteds (nowhere)	frampå (in front)
utfor (downhill)	tilbake (back)	overalt (everywhere)
innom (in)	utenlands (abroad)	kanskje (perhaps)

COMPARISON
The comparison of adverbs resembles that of adjectives:

Absolute	*Comparative*	*Superlative*
raskt (fast)	raskere (faster)	raskest (fastest)

Examples:
Paul går *raskt*. (Paul walks fast.)
Anne går *raskere* enn Paul. (Anne walks faster than Paul.)
Grete går *raskest*. (Grete walks the fastest.)

Irregular forms of comparison:

Absolute	*Comparative*	*Superlative*
bra/godt (well/good)	bedre (better)	best (best)
langt (far)	lenger	lengst
lenge (longer)	lenger	lengst
gjerne (gladly)	heller	helst
ille ⎫ (bad(ly))	verre	verst
vondt ⎭	verre/vondere	verst/vondest
dårlig (badly)	dårligere/verre	dårligst/verst
sjelden (rarely)	sjeldnere	sjeldnest

Absolute	Comparative	Superlative
mye/meget (much)	mer	mest
litt (a little)	mindre	minst
lite (little)	mindre	minst
nær (near)	nærmere	nærmest
tungt (heavily)	tyngre	tyngst
oppe (up)	lenger oppe	øverst
nede (below)	lenger nede	nederst
bak (behind)	lenger bak	bakerst
inne (inside)	lenger inne	innerst
ute (out)	lenger ute	ytterst
under (under)	lenger under	underst
borte (away)	lenger borte	bortest
midt ⎫ (middle)		midterst
mellom ⎭		mellomst
fram (forward, in front)	lenger fram	fremst
foran (in front)		forrest
nord (north)	lenger nord	nordligst
sør/syd (south)	lenger sør/syd	sørligst/sydligst
vest (west)	lenger vest	vestligst
øst (east)	lenger øst	østligst

Examples:

Du må stå lenger bak. (You must stand further back.)

Hvilken køye vil du ha? – Jeg vil ligge øverst. (Which bunk do you want? – I want the top one.)

Dine støvler står helt bakerst i skapet. (Your boots are right at the back of the cupboard.)

Some adverbs form the comparative and superlative with «mer» and «mest»:

a. Adverbs ending in -s:

gammeldags	mer gammeldags	mest gammeldags
(old-fashioned)	(more old-fashioned)	(most old-fashioned)
gradvis (gradually)	mer gradvis	mest gradvis

b. Participles used adverbially:

bitende (bitingly)	mer bitende	mest bitende

c. **Compound adverbs and adverbs with several syllables:**

selvsikkert   mer selvsikkert   mest selvsikkert
(self-confidently)

Adverbs fall into different categories according to their meanings:

Adverbs of degree

mye (much)	altfor/for (too)
meget/svært/veldig (very)	så (so)
enda (even)	neppe (hardly)
nokså (rather)	nesten (almost)
helt (completely)	bitende (bitingly, bitterly)
forferdelig (dreadfully)	aldeles (absolutely)
ganske (quite)	aller (by far, of all)

VELDIG, MEGET, SVÆRT, MYE, ENDA, ALLER

Den kaken er *veldig* god. (That cake is very good.)
Denne kaken er *mye* bedre. (This cake is much better.)
Denne kaken er *enda* bedre. (This cake is even better.)
Den der er *aller* best. (That one is the very best / the best of all.)

«Veldig», «meget» and «svært» must be accompanied by the absolute form of the adjective, «mye» and «enda» by the comparative form and «aller» by the superlative.

Adverbs of place

her (here)	herfra (from here)	ingensteds (nowhere)
der (there)	hvor (where)	tilbake (back)
nær (close, near)	innom (in)	nedi (down in)
overalt (everywhere)	noensteds (anywhere)	oppå (on top of)
derfra (from there)	utenlands (abroad)	hjem (home)

90

NOTE THE DIFFERENCE BETWEEN THE FOLLOWING PAIRS OF STATIVE AND DYNAMIC ADVERBS

a. At a place (stative)

Han *er*
- inne (in, inside, indoors)
- ute (out, outside, outdoors)
- oppe (upstairs)
- nede (downstairs)
- hjemme (at home)
- borte (away)
- framme (at his destination)
- vekk(e) (gone)
- her (here)
- der (there)

b. To a place (dynamic)

Han går
- inn (inside, in)
- ut (out, outside)
- opp (up, upstairs)
- ned (down, downstairs)
- hjem (home(-wards))
- bort (away)
- fram (forward)
- vekk (away)
- hit (here)
- dit (there)

PAIRS WITH THE SAME MEANINGS

The following pairs of words have the same meanings and can be used interchangeably.

ovenfra = ned fra (down from/from upstairs/from above)
nedenfra = opp fra (up from/from downstairs/from below)
østenfor = øst for (east of)
vestenfor = vest for (west of)
nordenfor = nord for (north of)
sønnenfor = sør for (south of)
bortenfor = lenger bort(e) enn (beyond)

Examples:
Han kom *neden(i)fra* [kjelleren]. (He came up [from the basement].)
Lyden kom *oven(i)fra*. (The noise came from upstairs.)

Adverbs of manner

hvordan (how)	sånn (so)	morsomt (amusingly)
hvorledes		
(how, in what way)	pent (prettily, nicely)	fort (quickly)
således (thus)	godt (well)	
slik (so)	hyggelig (pleasantly)	

SLIK/SÅNN – SLIKT/SÅNT
The adverb «slik/sånn» means «so, like that».
Example:
Du må ikke gjøre det *slik/sånn*. (You mustn't do it like that.)

Slik(t)/sånn/sånt can also be used adjectivally:
Examples:
et slikt/sånt hus (such a house)
en slik/sånn bil (such a car)

Wrong: Huset er slikt/sånt.

The correct form is:
Huset er slik/sånn (ie. the house is painted, decorated, built, designed like that, etc.)

HVORDAN
Hvordan har du det? (How are you?)
Han spør *hvordan* du har det. (He is asking how you are.)
Jeg vet ikke *hvordan* jeg skal gjøre det. (I don't know how to do it.)

Wrong: Jeg vet ikke hvordan å gjøre det

Adverbs of modification

ikke (not)	ellers (otherwise)	akkurat (exactly)
heller ikke		
(not . . . either)	visstnok (surely)	imidlertid (however)
kanskje (perhaps)	unektelig (undeniably)	sannsynlig(vis) (probably)

altså (therefore)	(al)likevel (anyway)	faktisk (in fact)
forresten (by the way)	også (also)	sikkert (surely)
riktignok (indeed)	bare (only)	jo (after all)
egentlig (really)	sannelig (certainly)	da (then)

DA, NOK, JO, VEL, NÅ, SIKKERT

These adverbs occur very frequently in everyday speech and are not always easy to translate. They are used to give an impression of doubt, caution and uncertainty, and are usually unstressed. The following examples may help to clarify their usage.

Han kommer *sikkert.* (He's bound to come. / I'm sure he'll come.)

Du er *vel* ferdig nå? (You are finished now, aren't you?)

> The use of «vel» here, accompanied by the appropriate intonation pattern, turns a basic statement into a question. The same applies to the adverbial phrase «ikke sant», which covers the vast majority of English tag questions (e.g. can't you, doesn't she, etc.).
> Example:
> Hun kommer i kveld, ikke sant? (She is coming tonight, isn't she?)

Kom *da!* (Come on then!)

> «Da» can often indicate impatience. In informal speech it can replace «vær så snill» to mean «please».

Han er *jo* norsk. (He is Norwegian, after all.)

As the following examples show, various combinations of these adverbs may occur. It is difficult to give definite rules for the correct sequence, but in general it is usual for the «lightest» to come first. Note that «ikke» (not) and «også» (also) always come at the end of a sequence of adverbs.

Jeg kan *nok dessverre ikke* komme. (I don't think I can come, unfortunately.)

Vi kan *da vanligvis ikke* gjøre det slik. (Well, we can't usually do it like that.)

Du kan *da vel ikke* mene det? (You can't really mean that?)

Han kunne *da vel også* hjelpe til litt? (Surely he could help a bit too?)

De kunne *nok sikkert også* klare det. (Surely they could manage it too.)

HELLER

«Heller» can have several different meanings:

1. **The comparative of «gjerne»:**
   gjerne – *heller* – helst
   Examples:
   Jeg vil *gjerne* ha vann. (I would like water.)
   Jeg vil *heller* ha melk enn vann. (I would rather have milk than water.)
   Jeg vil *helst* ha vin. (I would most prefer wine.)

2. Example:
   A. Marie sier: Jeg vil ha te.
      (Marie says: I want tea.)
      Per sier: Jeg vil også ha te.
      (Per says: I want tea too.)

   B. Marie sier: Jeg vil ikke ha kaffe.
      (Marie says: I don't want coffee.)
      Per sier: Jeg vil *heller ikke* ha kaffe.
      (Per says: I don't want coffee either.)

   As the examples above demonstrate, «også» in the positive sentence corresponds to *heller ikke* in the negative sentence.

   Wrong: Jeg vil også ikke ha kaffe.

   The correct form is: Jeg vil *heller ikke* ha kaffe.

   C. Marie (sier til Per):   Kan du komme?
       (Marie (says to Per):   Can you come?)
       Per svarer: Nei, dessverre.
       (Per replies: No, I'm afraid not.)
       Marie (sier til Ali):   Kan du komme da?
       (Marie (says to Ali):   Can you come, then?)
       Ali: Nei, *ikke* jeg *heller*.
                                    (No, I can't either.)
                                    Or: Nei, jeg kan *heller ikke* komme.
                                    (No, I can't come either.)

94

D. Marie:	Vil du heller ha cola?
	(Would you rather have a Coke?)
Per:	Nei, jeg vil *ikke* ha cola *heller*.
	(No, I don't want a Coke either.)

Adverbs of time

aldri (never)	nå (now)	sjelden (rarely)
alltid (always)	ofte (often)	lenge (a long time)
bestandig		
(constantly)	nettopp (just)	alt (already)
ennå (yet)	nylig (recently)	før (before)
da (then)	fremdeles (still)	allerede (already)
når (when)	snart (soon)	siden (since)
noen gang (ever)	så (then)	først (first)

ENNÅ – ENDA
Examples:
a. Båten har ikke kommet *ennå*. (The boat has not come yet.)
b. Det var *enda* dyrere i Tokyo enn i Oslo. (It was even more expensive in Tokyo than in Oslo.)
c. *Enda* det var ÷20 °C, gikk han uten jakke. (Even though it was minus 20 degrees Celsius, he went without a jacket.)
d. Han ville ha *enda* en kopp kaffe. (He wanted yet another cup of coffee.)

Usually «ennå» is used as an adverb of time and «enda» as an intensifier, but the latter is also used in modern spoken Norwegian in the sense of the former, even though this is not strictly correct.

DA – SÅ
Both «da» and «så» can be used as adverbs of time and as conjunctions.

Adverb of time:
Jeg ventet i to timer. *Da* kom han. (I waited for two hours. Then he came.)
Conjunction:
Vi gikk en tur i byen *da* han kom. (We went for a walk in the town when he came.)

95

Adverb of time:

Først snakket vi, *så* leste vi litt. (First we talked, then we read a little.)

Conjunction:

Kan du komme hit *så* vi kan snakke med deg? (Can you come here so we can talk to you?)

When «da» and «så» are used adverbially the verb phrase precedes the subject in the following clause.

NOEN GANG – NOEN GANGER

X: Har du *noen gang* vært i Afrika?
(Have you ever been to Africa?)

Y: Nei, jeg har aldri vært der.
(No, I've never been there.)

X: Har du *noen gang* hilst på kongen?
(Have you ever met the king?)

Y: Ja, jeg hilste på ham én gang utenfor slottet.
(Yes, I met him once outside the palace.)
Nå er han friskere enn *noen gang.*
(Now he's healthier than ever.)

«Noen gang» occupies the same place in the sentence as «aldri», «alltid», «sjelden», «ofte» and so on, and is used in interrogatives and with comparative structures.

«Noen ganger» (sometimes, a few times, several times) is placed at the beginning or the end of the clause:

Examples:
Jeg har vært der *noen ganger.* (I have been there a few times.)
Noen ganger er jeg i dårlig humør. (Sometimes I'm in a bad mood.)
Jeg har ikke vært der *noen ganger,* bare én gang. (I haven't been there several times, only once.)

Note the differences between the following sentences:
Har du *noen gang* snakket med henne? (Have you ever spoken to her?)
Har du snakket med henne *noen ganger*? (Have you spoken to her a few times?)
Har du ikke snakket med henne *noen gang*? (Haven't you ever spoken to her?)
Har du *aldri* snakket med henne? (Have you never spoken to her?)

SJELDEN – SJELDENT
Examples:

Adverb of time:
Han sang *sjelden.* (He sang rarely.)

Adverb of degree:
Det var en *sjelden/sjeldent* fin bil. (It was an unusually fine car.)
Det var et *sjelden/sjeldent* fint hus. (It was an uncommonly fine house.)

Adjective:
Det var et *sjeldent* frimerke. (It was a rare stamp.)
Det var en *sjelden* bil. (It was an unusual/rare car.)

FØRST
Examples:
Først spiste vi, så la vi oss. (First we ate, then we went to bed.)
Man ser problemet *først* når man begynner å bruke språket. (One can only see the problem when one starts to use the language.)

«bare» cannot be used as an adverb of time.
Det er *først* når de selv får barn, at de kan si noe om barneoppdragelse. (It's only when they have children of their own that they can talk about upbringing.)

«Først» is also the usual way of expressing «not until».
Example:
Hun kommer først kl 12. (She won't be here until 12 o'clock.)

Note also the following expression:
For det første var det dyrt, og *for det andre* likte jeg meg ikke der. (In the first place it was expensive, and in the second place I didn't like it there.)

Adverbial Phrases of Time

i går	i dag	i morgen
(yesterday)	(today)	(tomorrow)

i går morges	i morges	i morgen tidlig
(yesterday morning)	(this morning)	(tomorrow morning)
i går ettermiddag	i ettermiddag	i morgen ettermiddag
(yesterday afternoon)	(this afternoon)	(tomorrow afternoon)
i går kveld	i kveld	i morgen kveld
(yesterday evening)	(this evening)	(tomorrow evening)
i natt/natt til i dag	i natt	i morgen natt
(last night)	(tonight)	(tomorrow night)

Note: natt til torsdag (Wednesday night – **not** Thursday night!)

i forgårs		i over(i)morgen
(the day before yesterday)		(the day after tomorrow)
i fjor	i år	neste år
(last year)	(this year)	(next year)

i fjor vinter/sommer/vår/høst (last winter/summer/spring/autumn)
i vinter/sommer/vår/høst (this winter/summer/spring/autumn)
til vinteren/sommeren/våren/høsten (next winter/summer/
spring/autumn)

Examples:
I vinter skal jeg gå på ski. (This winter I'll go skiing: the winter is approaching.)
I vinter gikk jeg mye på ski. (This winter I went skiing a lot: the winter is over.)
I fjor vinter var det kaldt. (Last winter it was cold.)
Til vinteren skal jeg reise dit. (I'll go there next winter.)

OM SOMMEREN/VINTEREN/VÅREN/HØSTEN
a. Something which happens regularly each summer/winter/spring/autumn:
   Om høsten faller bladene av trærne. (In the autumn the leaves fall from the trees.)
   Om sommeren pleier jeg å ha ferie. (In the summer I usually have a holiday.)
b. In the sense of summer as opposed to other seasons:
   Han var her *om sommeren* det året. (He was here in the summer that year.)

OM DAGEN/NATTEN

a. In the sense of every day/night:
   Om dagen arbeider jeg. (During the day I work.)
b. In the sense of day as opposed to night:
   Han kjørte hit *om dagen* da han kom fra Bergen. (He drove here during the daytime when he came from Bergen.)
c. In the sense of «these days, at present»:
   Har du mye å gjøre *om dagen?* (Do you have a lot to do these days?)

I ÅR – I ÅRET

i år = this year:
I år tjener han godt. (This year he is earning well.)
i året = each year:
Han tjener kr 100 000 *i året.* (He earns 100.000 kroner a year.)

Note: To translate «this week», «this month», you must use
i denne uken (this week), *i denne måneden* (this month),
and **not** «i måned», etc. But *i uken* and *i måneden* are correct forms,
e.g.
Han tjener kr 4 000 *i måneden.* (He earns 4.000 kroner a month.)

DURATION OF TIME WITH DIFFERENT PREPOSITIONS

«For» in expressions of time (as in «for three years») can be
translated by three different prepositions in Norwegian:
1. *i:* in a positive sentence denoting duration.
2. *på:* in a negative sentence denoting duration.
3. *for:* when a pre-defined period is understood.

Examples:
1. Jeg har lest norsk *i tre år.* (I have studied Norwegian for 3 years.)

2. Jeg har ikke sett ham *på 3 år.* (I haven't seen him for 3 years.)

3. Jeg har leid huset *for tre år.* (I have rented the house for 3 years.)
   Han ble valgt til president *for tre år.* (He was elected president for 3 years.)

It can often be difficult to know when to use «for» and when to use
«i» in expressions such as these. In general, phrases of the type *for tre år* are the less common of the two.

Note also:

For . . . siden (. . . ago)

Han var her *for* tre år *siden*. (He was here 3 years ago.)

«In» can be translated in the following ways:

1. *Om:* after a given amount of future time has elapsed:

   Han kommer *om tre år*. (He is coming in three years.)

2. *På:* in the sense of «in the course of, within»:

   Du må gjøre arbeidet ferdig *på 3 år*. (You must finish the work in 3 years.)

«Om» is used for the future from the point of view of the present. For past time, «etter» is used:

Han kom tilbake *etter tre år*. (He came back after three years.)

HOLIDAYS

I juleferien:

I juleferien skal jeg gå på ski. (During the Christmas holidays I'm going skiing.)

I påskeferien:

I påskeferien skal vi på hytta. (During the Easter holidays we are going to our cabin.)

I ferien:

I ferien skal vi til Mallorca. (We're going to Mallorca for our holiday.)

I vinterferien:

I vinterferien skal vi være hjemme. (At half-term we'll stay at home.)

I julen:

I julen pleier vi å være hjemme. (At Christmas we usually stay at home.)

I påsken:

I påsken drar/drog mange til Hellas. (At Easter a lot of people go/went to Greece.)

But:

Om vinteren går vi på ski. (In the winter we go skiing.)

Wrong: Om påsken/julen/ferien.

Til jul:

Jeg fikk mange presanger til jul. (I got a lot of presents for Christmas.)

Jeg får vanligvis mange presanger til jul. (I usually get a lot of presents for Christmas.)

HOW LONG

Hvor lenge
Hvor lang tid } (How long)

Both expressions can often be used interchangeably for «how long»:

Hvor lenge
Hvor lang tid } har du vært i Norge?
(How long have you been in Norway?)

Hvor lenge
Hvor lang tid } skal du arbeide der?
(How long will you work there?)

Hvor lenge
Hvor lang tid } var du i India?
(How long were you in India?)

However, «hvor lenge» cannot normally be used with verbs used transitively:

Hvor lang tid tar reisen? (How long does the journey take?)
   (**Not** hvor lenge)

Hvor lang tid trenger du? (How long, = how much time, do you need?)
   (**Not** hvor lenge)

Hvor lang tid brukte du på det arbeidet? (How much time did you spend on that work?)
   (**Not** hvor lenge)

PRONOUNS

FORM:

The following paradigms show the systems of personal, reflexive and possessive pronouns in Norwegian.

Personal pronouns

	Subject form	Object form
SINGULAR		
1st person:	jeg (I)	meg (me)
2nd person:	du } (you) *De	deg } (you) *Dem
3rd person:	han (he)	ham (him)
	hun (she)	henne (her)
	den } (it) det	den } (it) det
PLURAL		
1st person:	vi (we)	oss (us)
2nd person:	dere } (you) *De	dere } (you) *Dem
3rd person:	de (they)	dem (them)

*Polite form.

Reflexive pronouns

SINGULAR

1st person:	meg (myself)
2nd person:	deg } (yourself) Dem
3rd person:	seg (himself/herself/itself/oneself)

PLURAL

1st person:	oss (ourselves)
2nd person:	dere ⎱ (yourselves) Dem ⎰
3rd person:	seg (themselves)

Possessive pronouns

REFERING TO SINGULAR NOUNS

	Masculine			Feminine	Neuter
1st sing.:	min		(my/mine)	mi	mitt
2nd sing.:	din Deres	⎱ (your/yours)		di Deres	ditt Deres
3rd sing.:	hans hennes dens dets	sin	(his/his) (her/hers) (its/–)	hans hennes｜si dens dets	hans hennes｜sitt dens dets

1st pl.:	vår		(our/ours)	vår	vårt
2nd pl.:	deres Deres		(your/yours)	deres Deres	deres Deres
3rd pl.:	deres ｜sin		(their/theirs)	deres ｜si	deres ｜sitt

REFERING TO PLURAL NOUNS

1st sing.:	mine	1st pl.:	våre
2nd sing.:	dine Deres	2nd pl.:	deres Deres
3rd sing.:	hans hennes｜sine dens dets	3rd pl.n:	deres ｜sine

Preliminary remarks

In the second person of all the pronouns, both singular and plural, two different forms have been given. The first form, written with a small *d*, is the so-called familiar form, whereas the second form, written with a capital *D*, is the polite form. To a certain degree it can be useful to compare «du», «deg», etc. and «De», «Dem», etc. with the French «tu» and «vous» or German «du» and «Sie»; however, the polite forms are used less and less in modern Norwegian, although in some

103

contexts it is still most natural to use them, especially for older people – for example to older strangers and in business correspondence. Examples:

Kjøpmannen: Kan jeg hjelpe *Dem* med noe? (The shopkeeper: Can I help you with anything?)

Politiet: Hvor bor *De?* (The police: Where do you live?)

Til en fremmed: Er det *Deres* hatt? (To a stranger: Is this your hat?)

FUNCTION

Personal pronouns

SUBJECT FORM

«Jeg», «du», «han», etc. are used as the subject of a clause:

Jeg skal ta en tur til byen. (I'm going to take a trip to town.)

Vil *du* være med? (Do you want to come?)

In certain informal contexts, «du» can be used to attract attention:

Du, hvor mange er klokka? (What time is it?)

In English, «du» here would often be replaced by the name of the person we are addressing, or an introductory phrase such as «by the way», «you know», etc.

SUBJECT OR OBJECT FORM

Either the subject or the object form of the pronoun can be used when it is placed predicatively:

Det er *meg*. / Det er *jeg*. (It's me.)

Han er større en *meg/jeg*. (He's bigger than me.)

The subject form is often preferred, however, when the pronoun is also the head of a relative clause:

Det var *dem/de* som gjorde det. (It was they who did it.)

Jeg så *dem/de* som skulle synge. (I saw the people who were going to sing.)

INDEFINITE USE – «DU», «DE»

«Du» and «de» can be used as indefinite pronouns, in the same way as «en», «man», corresponding to the indefinite use of «you», «they»:

Examples:
Du kan ikke få både i pose og sekk! (You can't have your cake and eat it!)
De sier at det går en fin film på kino nå. (They say there's a good film on at the cinema now.)

THE NEUTRAL FORMS «DEN», «DET»
The neutral forms are used in connection with animals and things, and agree in number and gender with the item they replace:
Examples:
Jeg har en hund. *Den* er tre år gammel. (I have a dog. It's three years old.)
På gården så jeg et lam, og *det* var så pent. (On the farm I saw a lamb, and it was so pretty.)
Der ligger det en bok. *Den* er min. (There is a book there. It's mine.)
Det står et glass der. *Det* er mitt. (There is a glass there. It's mine.)

REPETITION OF SUBJECT FORM
In modern spoken Norwegian you will often hear the subject repeated at the end of a sentence. This construction is used for the purpose of emphasis, or to make the sentence less formal or «rigid»:
Jeg var ikke enig med ham, *jeg*. (*I* didn't agree with him.)
Du kan godt gjøre det, *du*. (Why don't *you* do it.)

OBJECT FORM IN EXCLAMATIONS
Examples:
Stakkars meg! (Poor me!)
Kjære deg! (My dear!)
Dumme deg! (You silly (child, fool, etc.))
This construction occurs frequently in terms of endearment.

Reflexive pronouns

The reflexive pronouns occur in reflexive verbs, of which Norwegian has a considerable number. Some of these verbs have an equivalent reflexive meaning in English, such as:

å vaske seg (to wash (oneself))	å kose seg (to enjoy oneself)
å forsyne seg (to help oneself)	å kjøpe seg (to buy for oneself)

In other Norwegian reflexive verbs the reflexive meaning may not be so obvious.
Examples:

å like seg (to like (it), to feel at home)   å sette seg (to sit down)
å greie seg (to manage)   å ønske seg (to wish for)
å glede seg (to look forward to)   å finne seg (to put up with)
å grue seg (to dread)   å tenke seg (to imagine,
å vise seg (to appear, turn out)   consider)

COMPARISON WITH OBJECT FORM OF PERSONAL PRONOUNS

If one compares the reflexive pronouns with the object forms of the personal pronouns, only the third person forms vary. Note the differences between the following constructions:

Reflexive
Jeg vasker *meg*. (I wash myself.)
Han vasker *seg*. (He washes himself.)

Non-reflexive, with an object:
Jeg vasker *ham*. (I wash him.)
Han vasker *ham*. (He washes him.)

Many Norwegian verbs have both a reflexive and a non-reflexive form, though there is not necessarily any equivalence of meaning. The forms also behave differently in grammatical terms.
Examples:
å like seg: Jeg liker *meg* her. (I like it here, I feel at home here.)
å like: Jeg liker å bo her. (I like living here.)

Wrong: Jeg liker meg å bo her.

reflexive
↓
å glede seg: Jeg gleder *meg* til sommeren. (I'm looking forward to the summer.)

object
↓
å glede: Han gledet *meg* med vakker musikk. (He made me happy with beautiful music.)

INFINITIVES AFTER REFLEXIVE PRONOUNS

Normally the infinitive cannot occur directly after a reflexive pronoun, except in certain idioms such as:

skynde seg å gå (hurry up and go)
tenke seg å komme (consider coming)

Jeg ønsker *meg* en tur til Afrika. (I would like a trip to Africa.)
Jeg ønsker å ta en tur til Afrika. (I would like to take a trip to Africa.)

Wrong: Jeg ønsker meg å ta en tur til Afrika.

Possessive pronouns

The possessive pronouns decline according to the number and gender of the noun to which they refer. Some persons of the possessive pronouns have the same form regardless of whether they refer to a masculine, neuter, singular or plural noun – for example «hans» (his), «hennes» (her), «Deres» (your).

In contrast to English, the emphatic form of the possessive pronoun in Norwegian is identical to the non-emphatic form. Thus, while in English two distinct forms exist, for example «my» and «mine», Norwegian has only one form for both constructions.

Examples:

Jeg bor i huset mitt. Huset er *mitt.*
(I live in my house.) (The house is mine.)

Wrong: Huset er mine.

Hun holder veska si/sin veske. Veska er *hennes.*
(She is holding her bag.) (The bag is hers.)
Han kjører bilen sin/sin bil. Bilen er *hans.*
(He is driving his car.) (The car is his.)
Vi bor i en ny leilighet. Leiligheten er *vår.*
(We live in a new flat.) (The flat is ours.)
De bor i et stort hus. Huset er *deres.*
(They live in a big house.) (The house is theirs.)
Jeg liker kattene mine/mine katter. Kattene er *mine.*
(I like my cats.) (The cats are mine.)

POSITION

Another peculiarity is that the non-emphatic possessive pronouns can often either be placed before the noun, as in English, or after the noun. The latter construction is more common in colloquial speech. Note that in this construction the noun is always in the definite form. Examples:

Jeg leste i *boka mi.* (I was reading my book)

Har du hilst på *mannen min?* (Have you met my husband?)

Har du sett den nye *leiligheten deres?* (Have you seen their new flat?)

In certain set phrases, the possessive pronoun will always precede the noun

Det er ikke *min skyld.* (It's not my fault.)

I *vår tid* snakkes det mye om forurensning. (These days there is a lot of talk about pollution.)

I *mine øyne* er han en helt. (In my view he's a hero.)

When «egen» (own) is used in conjunction with a noun, the possessive pronoun is placed first

Jeg sov i *min egen seng.* (I slept in my own bed.)

Vi bodde i *vårt eget hus.* (We lived in our own house.)

When a noun is preceded by an adjective, the possessive pronoun is usually placed finally

De fine blomstene hennes ble solgt på torget. (Her lovely flowers were sold at the market.)

Hun likte *det nye slipset hans.* (She liked his new tie.)

Jeg tok med meg *den nye boka mi.* (I took my new book with me.)

Den lille gutten hennes var syk. (Her little boy was ill.)

The alternative forms

    hennes fine blomster . . .

    hans nye slips . . .

    min nye bok . . .

    hennes lille gutt . . .

are also correct, but are less common in everyday speech.

The possessive pronoun normally comes last in clauses with «alle», «alt», «all» and «hele»

Hun vasket *alt tøyet deres*. (She washed all their clothes.)
Hunden spiste opp *all maten vår*. (The dog ate up all our food.)
Jeg brukte opp *hele lønnen min* på en dag. (I spent all my wages in one day.)

However, the possessive pronoun is placed immediately before the noun in certain idioms:
Jeg har slitt *i all min dag*. (I have worked hard all my life.)
Jeg har aldri vært syk *i hele mitt liv*. (I have never been ill all my life.)

GENITIVE EXPRESSIONS INVOLVING A PRONOUN

In the chapter on nouns, we saw that most genitive constructions can also be expressed using a preposition, for example:
Alis hus (Ali's house)   →   huset til Ali

Note, however, that in genitive expressions involving a pronoun, the prepositional construction cannot be used:

Wrong: Huset til ham/han er i Oslo.

The only correct alternatives are:
huset hans and *hans hus*:
Huset hans / Hans hus er i Oslo. (His house is in Oslo.)

Reflexive possessive pronouns

1. If the subject and the owner are one and the same person, and we are referring to a subject in the third person, either singular or plural, the reflexive possessive pronoun «sin», «si», «sitt» or «sine» is used. The reflexive possessive pronouns also decline according to the number and gender of the noun they refer to. Examples:
   Henry tar sykkelen *sin*. (Henry takes his bicycle, ie. his own.)
   Henry tar sykkelen *hans*. (Henry takes his bicycle, ie. someone else's.)

109

Henry og Per tar syklene *sine*. (Henry and Per take their bicycles, ie. their own.)

Odd og Kari tar syklene *deres*. (Odd and Kari take their bicycles, ie. two other people's bicycles.)

Odd snakker med kona *hans*. (Odd is speaking to his wife, ie. someone else's wife.)

Odd snakker med Kari, kusinen *sin*. (Odd is speaking to Kari, his cousin; ie. his own.)

But note: Odd snakker med Kari, som er kusinen *hans*. (Odd is speaking to Kari, who is his cousin, ie. his own.)

The last example illustrates a feature which often presents considerable difficulty when learning Norwegian. The main rule is that «sin», «si», «sitt» and «sine» can only be used when the subject/«owner» and object/«owned» *occur in one and the same clause*. As soon as the next clause begins, be it a relative clause or any other form of subordinate or coordinate clause, the non-reflexive possessive pronoun is used. Here are some further examples:

Hun hentet *sin* datter Kari fra flyplassen.

Hun sa at *hennes* datter Kari var kommet hjem.

(«hennes datter Kari» is the subject of the subordinate clause.)

2. **«Sin», «sitt», «si» and «sine» cannot be used as the subject of a sentence.**

Henry tar sykkelen sin. Sykkelen *hans* er fransk. (Henry is taking his bicycle. His bicycle is French.)

Wrong: Sykkelen sin er fransk.

Also in coordinated subjects, it is incorrect to use «sin», «sitt», etc.:

Per bor sammen med *kona si*. Per og *kona hans* bor sammen. (Per lives with his wife. Per and his wife live together.)

Wrong: Per og kona si bor sammen.

3. a. «sin», «sitt», «si» and «sine» cannot be used predicatively in a simple sentence (se also 3c below)

110

Examples:
Hvem er det? Det er broren til Henry. (Who is that? It's Henry's brother.)
Det er *broren hans.* (It's his brother.)

Wrong: Det er broren sin.

Han vasker klærne sine. Det er *klærne hans.* (He is washing his clothes. They are his clothes.)

Wrong: Det er klærne sine.

Det er *huset hans.* Huset er *hans.* (It is his house. The house is his.)

Wrong: Huset er sitt. Det er huset sitt.

b. **In comparisons, «sin», «sitt», «si» and «sine» are used.**
   Examples:
   Hun er mindre enn *broren sin.* (She is smaller than her brother.)
   Hun er like liten som *broren sin.* (She is as small as her brother.)
   Han er eldre enn *kusinene sine.* (He is older than his cousins.)
   Hun er lik *sin mor* (= hun likner *sin mor.*) (She is like her mother.)

c. **Emphasis:**
   Han vasker *klærne sine.* Det er *klærne sine* han vasker. (He is washing his (own) clothes. It's his (own) clothes he's washing.)

   Here, the object of the main clause receives the focus of the sentence, a device often used for emphasis.
   Example:
   De passer *barnet sitt.* Det er *barnet sitt* de passer. (They are looking after their (own) child. It's their (own) child they are looking after.)
   (See also the section on cleft sentences.)

4. Grammatical and logical subject

With verbs such as «be» (ask), «la» (let), «tillate» (permit, allow), the pronoun may refer back to the logical subject rather than to the grammatical subject.

Examples:

Foreldrene ba dem (barna) hente *klærne sine*. (The parents asked them (the children) to fetch their clothes.)

Who owns the clothes?

Either:

1. The parents, if *sine* refers to the grammatical subject.

Or:

2. Them (the children), if *sine* refers to the logical subject.

Such ambiguity can be avoided by using constructions such as:

Foreldrene sa at barna skulle hente *klærne sine*. (The parents said that the children should fetch their (own) clothes.)

where «barna» (the children) is both the grammatical and the logical subject of the relative clause.

5. Special idioms

«Sin», «sitt», «si» and «sine» are used in some special idioms where the pronoun does not necessarily refer to a specific subject.

Examples:

Det var *jenta si!* (There's a good girl!)

Til sine tider kan det være vanskelig. (At times things can be difficult.)

I sin tid var jeg leder for denne gruppen. (At one time I was the leader of this group.)

Demonstrative pronouns

Norwegian has two main demonstrative pronouns, corresponding to *this/these* and *that/those,* which inflect for number and gender.

FORM:

Masc./Fem.:	den (that)	–	denne (this)
Neuter:	det (that)	–	dette (this)
Plural:	de (those)	–	disse (these)

112

Examples:

Denne koppen er stor, men *den* koppen er liten. (This cup is big, but that cup is small.)

Han ville kjøpe *denne* store koppen, men hun ville ha *den* lille koppen der. (He wanted to buy this big cup, but she wanted to have that small cup there.)

Denne er stor, men *den* er liten. (This one is big, but that one is small.)

Hun ville ha *den* der. (She wanted that one there.)

Note that Norwegian does not translate «one» as in «this one», «that one», etc.

OBLIGATORY NEUTER SINGULAR FORM

Where in English this/that/these/those is the subject of the verb *to be* with a following noun in the predicate, in Norwegian the neuter singular form of the pronoun («det», «dette») is always used, regardless of the number and gender of the subsequent noun.
Examples:

Det(te) er en stor kopp. (That/this is a big cup.)

Det(te) er den store koppen. (That/this is the big cup.)

Wrong: Den(ne) er en stor kopp. Den(ne) er den store koppen.

Det(te) er en pen bok. (That/this is a nice book.)
Det(te) er den pene boka. (That/this is the nice book.)
Det(te) er et nytt skap. (That/this is a new cupboard.)
Det(te) er det nye skapet. (That/this is the new cupboard.)
Det(te) er gode bøker. (Those/these are good books.)
Det(te) er de gode bøkene. (Those/these are the good books.)
Det(te) er nye skap. (Those/these are new cupboards.)
Det(te) er de nye skapene. (Those/these are the new cupboards.)

DEFINITE ARTICLE OR DEMONSTRATIVE PRONOUN?

When an adjective precedes the noun, it is impossible to see the difference between the definite article and the demonstrative pronoun.

Examples:

Without adjective:

Definite article	*Demonstrative pronoun*
stol*en*	*den* stolen / *denne* stolen
(the chair)	(that chair / this chair)

With adjective:

den gode stolen	*den* gode stolen / *denne* gode stolen
(the good chair)	(that good chair / this good chair)

Wrong: gode stolen

In the sentence «Den gode stolen vil jeg ha», the only distinction between the definite article «den» (the) and the demonstrative pronoun «den» (that) is the stress. The latter carries stress, whereas the former is always unstressed.

In certain contexts the demonstrative pronoun can be strongly stressed to emphasize a quality or degree:

Hun hadde *den* fine kjolen! (She had such a fine dress!)

COMPOUND/SIMPLE DEFINITE

Normally the demonstrative pronoun governs the compound definite form of the noun:

denne tank*en* (this thought),

though in some cases the simple definite form is also permissible. See the section on the Articles.

SPECIAL NOTE ON DEMONSTRATIVE PRONOUNS

a. **«Det»/«dette» can refer to an entire phrase:**

Han prøvde å smugle inn vin, men *det* gikk ikke. (He tried to smuggle wine in, but that didn't work.)

Han snakket stygt til henne og hånte henne, alt *dette* fordi hun hadde sviktet ham. (He spoke roughly to her and mocked her, all because she had betrayed him.)

b. **The use of «denne», «disse» and «dette» can in some contexts have a negative implication:**

Hva vil de, disse politikerne? (What do they want, these politicians?)

Hva betyr det egentlig, dette her? (What does this really mean?)

OTHER DEMONSTRATIVE PRONOUNS

1. **slik/sånn**
   slikt/sånt } (such)
   slike/sånne

   «Slik» and «sånn», with their inflected forms, are synonyms.
   Examples:
   Har du hørt *slikt/sånt* bråk? (have you ever heard such (a) noise?)
   Slike/sånne oppgaver liker jeg. (I like such exercises / exercises like that.)
   En *slik/sånn* kjole vil jeg ha. (I want such a dress / a dress like that.)

2. **samme** (same)
   Examples:
   De kjører *samme* vei / *samme* veien / den *samme* veien. (They drive the same way.)
   Dagsrevyen kommer på *samme* tid hver dag. (The News is at the same time each day.)
   De tar (den) samme buss(en) hver dag. (They take the same bus each day.)

   Do not confuse «samme» (same) and «sammen» (together):
   De bor *sammen*. (They live together.)
   De bor i *samme* hus. (The live in the same house.)

3. **selv** (self)
   a. «Selv» as an indeclinable reflexive pronoun after a noun, meaning «himself», «herself», «themselves», etc.
      Examples:
      Paven *selv* var der. (The Pope himself was there.)
      Jeg skal hente det *selv*. (I shall fetch it myself.)
      Note the various possibilities for the positioning of «selv» in the sentence:
      Skal jeg gjøre det for deg? (Shall I do it for you?)
      – Nei, jeg kan gjøre det *selv*.
      – Nei, jeg kan *selv* gjøre det. } (No, I can do it myself.)
      – Nei, jeg *selv* kan gjøre det.

   b. «Selv» + e when used adjectivally before a noun in the singular means «in person», «proper».

Examples:
Selve paven var der. (The pope was there in person.)
Det er mange parkeringsplasser i *selve* Oslo. (There are many car-parks in Oslo proper.)

Note that «selve» cannot be used in conjunction with nouns in the plural.

Wrong: selve kvinner

«Selve» has also a superlative form, «selveste», which has much the same meaning as its absolute counterpart, only with a stronger emphasis:
Jeg så til og med *selveste* paven! (I even saw the Pope himself!)

c. «Selv» can also function adverbially to mean «even», and is then always placed at the beginning of a clause:
Selv paven var der. (Even the Pope was there.)
Selv jeg kan gjøre det. (Even I can do that.)
Jeg fortalte ham at *selv* min bror kunne klare det. (I told him that even my brother could manage that.)

4. **begge** (both)
   a. can be used adjectivally, preceding a noun:
   begge guttene (both the boys)
   begge steder (both places)

   b. can be combined with «to», without a following noun:
   Vil du ha dette eplet eller den pæren? Jeg vil ha *begge to*. (Do you want this apple or that pear? I want both (of them).)

   Wrong: Jeg vil ha begge to fruktene

   But: «Jeg vil ha begge fruktene» (I want both the fruits) is correct.

   c. In conjunction with a personal pronoun:
   Vi kan *begge* komme. (We can both come.)
   Alternatively:
   Vi kan komme *begge to*.

d. *Begge to – begge deler*

«Begge to» is used with two specific items of a similar kind (except in the case of proper names).
Examples:
Kjenner du Kari eller Knut? *Begge to.* (Do you know Kari or Knut? Both of them.)
Vil du ha eplet eller pæren? *Begge to.* (Do you want the apple or the pear? Both (of them).)
Vil du ha den lille eller den store flasken? *Begge to.* (Do you want the small or the large bottle? Both (of them).)

«Begge deler» has a more general reference, when the nouns to which it refers are in the indefinite form.
Examples:
Snakker du norsk eller engelsk? *Begge deler.* (Do you speak Norwegian or English? Both.)
Liker du spaghetti eller poteter? *Begge deler.* (Do you like spaghetti or potatoes? Both.)

«Både . . . og» (both . . . and) can be used in all the examples above:
både eplet og pæren (both the apple and the pear), både Kari og Knut (both Kari and Knut), både spaghetti og poteter (both spaghetti and potatoes).
«Både» must always be followed by «og». Note that «både . . . og» can in Norwegian be used to refer to more than two things, for example:
Både epler, pærer *og* druer (Apples, pears and grapes), whereas in English *both* must always refer to no more nor less than two items.

Interrogative Pronouns

Hvem (who)
Hva (what)
Hvilken/hvilket/hvilke (which)
Hva for en/et/noe/noen (what/which)

HVEM

a. refers to people and can be both subject and object.
   Examples:
   Hvem er det? (Who is it?)
   Han spør *hvem* det er. (He asks who it is.)
   Hvem skriver du til? / Til *hvem* skriver du? (Who are you writing to? / To whom are you writing?)
   Hvem liker du best, Arne eller Tor? (Whom do you like best, Arne or Tor?)
   Hvem kan komme? *Hvem* som helst. (Who can come? Anybody.)
   Hvem eier denne boka? (Who owns this book? Whose book is this?)

   «Whose» can also be rendered in several other ways. In colloquial Norwegian the following construction is frequently used:
   Hvem er det sin bok? (Whose book is that?)
   Hvem er det sitt hus? (Whose house is that?)

   Note also:
   Mannen, som jeg hadde lånt boken av, var norsk. (The man whose book I had borrowed was Norwegian.)

b. Remember that «hvem» cannot occur directly in relation to a noun:

   Wrong: Hvem gutt er det?

   The correct form is
   Hvilken gutt er det? (Which boy is that?)
   or
   Hvem er den gutten? (Who is that boy?)

HVA

a. cannot refer to people, only inanimate objects.
   Examples:
   Hva vil du? (What do you want?)
   Han spør *hva* du vil. (He asks what you want.)
   Fortell alt *hva* du vet. (Relate everything that you know.)
   Hva tenker du på? (What are you thinking?)
   Han spør *hva* du tenker på. (He is asking what you're thinking.)
   Hva kan jeg ta? *Hva* som helst. (What can I take? Anything.)

b. In certain set phrases «hva» can occur with a noun.
Examples:
Hva slags: *Hva slags* filmer liker du best? (What sort of films do you like best?)
Hva nytte: *Hva nytte* kan vi ha av det? (What use is that to us?)
   The more common expression is «hvilken» nytte.

Wrong: Hva filmer liker du best?

The correct alternatives are: *Hva slags* filmer / *hvilke* filmer . . .

c. Idiomatic expressions
Examples:
Vet du hva, nå kan jeg snakke litt norsk. (Guess what – now I can speak some Norwegian.)
Nei, *vet du hva!* (Stop it, that's enough!)
Han er gjerrig og, *hva verre er,* han er uærlig. (He's mean and, what's worse, he's dishonest.)
Hva meg angår, så spiller det ingen rolle. (As far as I'm concerned it doesn't matter.)

HVILKEN, HVILKET, HVILKE

inflect for number and gender, can refer to both people and things, and normally precede the noun in the indefinite form.
Examples:
Hvilken buss kan jeg ta? (Which bus can I take?)
Du kan ta *hvilken som helst* (buss). (You can take any (bus).)

Wrong: Hvilken bussen.

Hvilket hus bor du i? / I *hvilket* hus bor du? (Which house do you live in? / In which house do you live?)
Hvilke epler er best? (Which apples are best?)

In the expression «which one», *one* is not translated in Norwegian.

HVA FOR EN / ET / NOE / NOEN

often replace «hvilken», «hvilket», «hvilke» in everyday speech.
Examples:
Hvilken buss tar du? / *Hva for en* buss tar du?

The distinction between these two constructions can best be illustrated by which/what in English:
Which bus do you take / What bus do you take, where the latter is more colloquial.
Hvilket hus / *Hva for et* hus bor du i? (Which house / What house do you live in?)
Hvilke epler er best? / *Hva* for noen epler er best? (Which/what apples are best?)
Note the expressions:
Hva for noe? (What?)
and
Hva sa du *for noe?* (What did you say?)
which are very common in everyday, informal usage.

Relative pronouns

SOM
(who, which, that)
is the most frequently used relative pronoun in modern Norwegian, and occurs both as subject and object. Normally «som» refers to the noun or pronoun immediately preceding it.
Examples:
Den gutten *som* går der, er broren min. (The boy who is walking there is my brother.)
Jeg hilste på henne *som* besøkte oss i fjor. (I said hello to the girl / woman etc. who visited us last year.)

The construction where the relative pronoun refers back to an object pronoun is very uncommon in English, but much more usual in Norwegian.
Note also the following example:
Jeg så *dem/de* som skulle synge. (I saw the people who were going to sing.)
In English we must use a noun, not a pronoun.

Det var jeg, *som* måtte gjøre det. (It was I who had to do it.)
Der står den sengen *som* skulle males. (There is the bed which was going to be painted.)

As in English, «som» can be omitted when it does not refer to the subject of the sentence.

Examples:

Den gutten *(som)* du ser der, er broren min. (The boy (whom) you see there is my brother.)

Vi spiste den maten *(som)* Tor hadde laget. (We ate the food (which) Tor had made.)

Sengen *(som)* du sover i, er hundre år gammel. (The bed (which) you are sleeping in is 100 years old.)

Det var Per *(som)* hun ikke ville treffe. (It was Per (whom) she didn't want to meet.)

Wrong: Den gutten, hvem går der, er broren min. Senga, at du ligger i . . .

«Som» can also refer to entire phrases or clauses, similar to «something» in English, in which case «noe» is often added before the relative pronoun or instead of it. «Hva» can also take the place of the combination «noe som» in these constructions.

Examples:

Jeg har gått på kurs, *noe (som)* du også burde gjøre.
(I have been on a course, something you ought to do too.)

Hun er alltid så sulten, *noe (som)* jeg ikke kan forstå.
(She is always so hungry, something I can't understand.)

Han kan bake brød, *noe (som)* jeg ikke kan.
(He can bake bread, something I can't do.)

SUBJECT IN RELATIVE CLAUSES

When «hvem», «hva» or «hvilken»/«hvilket»/«hvilke» is the subject of a relative clause, «som» is obligatory.

Examples:

Hvem kommer? (Who is coming?)
↑
SUBJECT

Jeg vet ikke *hvem som* kommer.
(I don't know who's coming.)

Hvem bad hun? (Who did she invite?)
Jeg vet ikke hvem hun bad. (I don't know whom she invited.)

Hva er i veien? (What's wrong?)
↑
SUBJECT

Jeg vet ikke *hva som* er i veien.
(I don't know what's wrong.)

Hva vil han? (What does he want?)
Jeg vet ikke hva han vil. (I don't know what he wants.)

Hvilken selges mest? (Which one is sold most?)
↑
SUBJECT

Jeg vet ikke *hvilken som* selges mest.
(I don't know which one is sold most.)
Hvilken selger du mest av? (Which one do you sell most of?)
Jeg vet ikke hvilken jeg selger mest av. (I don't know which one I sell most of.)

SPECIAL USES OF «SOM»

a. *Som ung* var hun ivrig idrettsjente. (As a young girl she was a keen athlete.)
   Som liten bodde han på landet. (When he was little he lived in the country.)

b. Hun arbeidet *som* lege i Finnmark. (She worked as a doctor in Finnmark.)

c. *Som* ingeniør bør du vite dette. (As an engineer, you should know this.)

d. Han snakket til meg *som* til et barn. (He spoke to me as he would to a child.)
   Som du sår, skal du høste. (As a man sows, so shall he reap.)

e. Hun er like gammel ⎫
      likså gammel ⎬ *som* meg.
      så gammel ⎭
   (She is the same age as me.)

f. Hun er slik *som* meg. (She is like me.)

g. Hva skal jeg gjøre? *Hva som helst.* (What shall I do? Anything.)
Hvor skal vi gå? *Hvor som helst.* (Where shall we go?
Anywhere.)
Hvem skal vi be? *Hvem som helst.* (Whom shall we invite?
Anyone/anybody.)
Hvilken buss vil du ta? *Hvilken som helst.* (Which bus will you
take? Any.)

LITERARY FORMS
In older Norwegian literature the forms «hvis», «hvem», «hva»,
«hvilken»/«hvilket»/«hvilke» will occasionally be found instead of
the relative pronoun «som».
Examples:
Det er et menneske i *hvem* det ikke er svik. (That is a person in
whom there is no betrayal.)
In modern idiom this sentence would normally read:
Det er et menneske *som* det ikke er svik i.

Det dannet seg store køer foran teatret, *hvilket* ofte skjer ved store
premierer. (Long queues formed outside the theatre, something
which often happens at big premières.)
More colloquially: . . . foran teatret, *og dette* skjer ofte ved . . .
Or: . . . foran teatret, *noe som* ofte skjer ved . . .

Mannen, *hvis* navn jeg ikke husker, ønsket å hilse på fruen. (The
man, whose name I do not remember, wished to meet the lady.)
Colloquially: Jeg husker ikke navnet på mannen som ønsket . . .

CLEFT SENTENCES
A part of a sentence can be given extra emphasis by removing it
from the original sentence and making it the focal point of its own
relative clause.
Examples:
Jeg mente det. (I meant that.)
Det var *det (som)* jeg mente. (That was what I meant.)
«Det var hva jeg mente» can also be heard.

Jeg ville det. (I wanted that.)
Det var *jeg som* ville det. (It was I who wanted that.)

Det var *det (som)* jeg ville. (It was that I wanted. / That was what I wanted.)

Hun gjorde det. (She did that.)
Det var *hun som* gjorde det. (It was she who did that.)
Det var *det (som)* hun gjorde. (That was what she did.)

Han sa det. (He said it.)
Det var *han som* sa det. (It was he who said it.)
Det var *det (som)* han sa. (That was what he said.)

Han kom. (He came.)
Det var *han som* kom. (It was he who came.)

Jeg elsket henne som satt der. (I loved the girl who was sitting there.)
Det var *henne, som* satt der, som jeg elsket. (It was the girl who sat there whom I loved.)

Jeg mente ham. (I meant him.)
Det var *ham (som)* jeg mente. (It was him I meant. / He was the one I meant.)

Wrong: Det var hvem jeg mente.

«SOM» IN RELATION TO TIME AND PLACE
In some cases «som» can have the same function as an adverb of time or place.
Examples:
Nå *som* vinteren kommer . . . (Now that winter is coming . . .)
De steder *som* vi har vært på . . . (The places where we have been . . .)
Der *som* vi har vært . . . (Where we have been . . .)
Det året *som* jeg kom hit . . . (The year in which I came here . . .)
I huset *som* han bodde i . . . (In the house in which he lived . . .)

Reciprocal pronouns

HVERANDRE
(each other)
is the reciprocal pronoun used in modern Norwegian, usually referring to a plural subject.
Examples:
De elsket *hverandre*. (They loved each other.)
Vi har møtt *hverandre* før. (We have met each other before.)
Dere må hjelpe *hverandre*. (You must help each other.)
It is important not to confuse the reciprocal and the reflexive pronouns.

Wrong: Vi har møtt oss før.

Occasionally «hverandre» can refer to a subject which is grammatically singular but logically plural.
Examples:
Brudeparet kysset *hverandre* foran fotografene. (The bride and groom kissed (each other) in front of the photographers.)
Hele *klassen* hadde lært *hverandre* å kjenne. (The whole class had got to know each other.)

Indefinite pronouns

EN, MAN
«One» is rendered in Norwegian by «en»/«man», which can be used interchangeably as the subject of a clause.
Examples:
Man/En kan ikke få alt her i verden. (One can't have everything in life.)
Man/En lærer så lenge *man/en* lever. (One lives and learns.)

However, only «en» can be used in object position or in the genitive form:
Kurset krever mye av *en*. (The course demands a lot of one.)

Wrong: . . . mye av man.

Ens beste venner kan ofte glemme *en*. (One's best friends can often forget one.)

125

Assertive pronouns

NOEN, NOE
(some/any, somebody – some/any, something)
«Noen» and «noe» can either modify a noun, or they can stand on
their own.

Masculine/feminine singular
Har du *noen* idé? (Do you have any idea?)
Jeg har *ikke noen* idé. (I have no idea. / I don't have any idea.)

Wrong: Jeg har noen idé.

Det er *noen* her. (There's somebody here.)

Masculine/feminine plural
Jeg har *noen* idéer. (I have some ideas.)
Har du *noen* idéer? (Do you have any ideas?)
Jeg har *ikke noen* idéer. (I have no ideas. / I don't have any ideas.)
Det er *noen* her. (There are some (people) here.)

Neuter singular
Har dere *noe* sted å bo? (Do you have anywhere to live?)
Vi har *ikke noe* sted å bo. (We don't have anywhere to live. / We
have nowhere to live.)

Wrong: Jeg har noe sted å bo.

Det er *noe* her. (There's something here.)

Neuter plural
Jeg har *noen* bilder. (I have some pictures?)
Har du *noen* bilder? (Do you have any pictures?)
Jeg har *ikke noen* bilder. (I don't have any pictures. / I have no
pictures.)
Det er *noen* her. (There are some here.)

Mass nouns
Har du *noe* mat? (Do you have some/any food?)
Jeg har *noe* mat. (I have some food.)
Jeg har ikke *noe* mat. (I don't have any food. / I have no food.)

The above paradigm illustrates that the plural form is always «noen», regardless of gender, but that «noen» can also be used in the masculine and feminine singular in interrogative and negative sentences.
«Noe» is always used for an unspecified amount of something, regardless of the noun's gender:
noe mat (some food), *noe* vann (some water), *noe* bagasje (some luggage), *noe* smør (some butter), etc.,
and also in the neuter singular in interrogative and negative sentences.

ANNEN, ANNET, ANDRE
Note the following expressions using «annen», «annet», «andre»:
Jeg så *et eller annet* der borte. (I saw something or other over there.)
En eller annen har vært her. (Someone or other has been here.)
fra det ene til det andre (from one thing to another)
Du kan sove, mens *en annen* må jobbe! (You can sleep, while some of us have to work!)
Det var *noe annet!* (That was something else again!)

MANGE, MYE, MANG EN, MANGT ET
(much, many)
See the chapter on adjectives for descriptions of the form and function of «mye» (much) and «mange» (many). There are in addition two other pronouns in this class, «mang en» (masc./fem.) and «mangt et» (neut.), but these are less frequent in modern Norwegian usage. They correspond to the English «many a . . .» and govern a noun in the singular. They occur mainly in a few set phrases:
Mang en gang har jeg ønsket meg en tur til Spania. (Many a time I've wished for a trip to Spain.)
Jeg har *mangt et minne* fra barndommen. (I have many a recollection from my childhood.)
De hadde *mangt* å snakke om. (They had much to talk about.)

Negative pronouns

INGEN, INGENTING, IKKE NOEN, IKKE NOE
«Ingen» means the same as «ikke noen» (no, no-one, nobody).
«Ingenting» means the same as «ikke noe» (nothing), except where

«ikke noe» means «no, not any» before a neuter knoun. As the *subject* of a clause they are interchangeable.
Examples:

Ingen
Ikke noen } hjelper dem. (Nobody helps them.)

Ingenting
Ikke noe } hjelper. (Nothing helps.)

Han sier at *ingen / ikke noen* har hjulpet dem. (He says that nobody had helped them.)

But: *Ikke noe* hotell er bra nok for ham. (No hotel is good enough for him.)

However, as an *object* they are not always interchangeable:
1. *Main clause, simple verb:*
   Jeg har *ingen / ikke noen* bok. (I have no book. / I do not have a book.)
   Jeg sa *ingenting / ikke noe*. (I said nothing. / I did not say anything.)
   Jeg har *ikke noe* sted å bo. (I have nowhere to live.)

2. *Main clause, compound verb:*
   Jeg har *ikke* sett *noen* bil som jeg har likt. (I haven't seen any car that I have liked.)
   Jeg har *ikke* sett *noe* hus som jeg har likt. (I haven't seen any house that I have liked.)
   Jeg har *ikke* sagt *noe*. (I haven't said anything.)

   Wrong: Jeg har sett ingen bil. Jeg har sagt ingenting.

   Jeg passer *ikke* på *noen*. (I look after no-one. / I don't look after anyone.)

   Wrong: Jeg passer på ingen.

3. *Subordinate clause:*
   Han sa at han *ikke* hadde sett *noen* bil som han likte. (He said that he hadn't seen any car that he liked.)
   Han sa at han *ikke* hadde sett *noe* hus som han likte. (He said that he hadn't seen any car that he liked.)
   Han sa at han *ikke* hadde sagt *noe*. (He said that he hadn't said anything.)

Wrong: Han sa at han hadde kjøpt ingen bil. Han sa at han hadde sagt ingenting.

Universal pronouns

ALL, ALT, ALLE, ALLTING
(all, everything)
a. «All» and «alt» are used to modify mass nouns. «Alt» can also occur on its own (often followed by «sammen»), or can be replaced by «allting».
Examples:
Hun lagde *all* maten selv. (She cooked all the food herself.)
Hun lagde *alt* (sammen) selv. (She cooked it all herself.)
Hun gjorde *allting/alt* selv. (She did everything herself.)
Alt stoffet skulle selges på salg. (All the material was going to be sold in the sale.)
Alt skal selges ut. (Everything is going in the sale.)

b. «Alle» precedes a noun in the plural, and can also occur on its own, or with «sammen», when referring to a plural noun or noun phrase.
Examples:
Alle barna kunne lese. (All the children could read.)
Alle (sammen) kunne lese. (All of them could read.)
Han brukte opp *alle* pengene sine. (He spent all his money.)

Note that in Norwegian, «of» (as in the expression «all of . . .») is never translated. «Alle» stands alone without a Norwegian equivalent of «of them».

c. Normally «all», «alt», «alle» require the noun to be in the definite form; however, the indefinite form is correct in general references.
Examples:
All bagasje må ekspederes før avreise. (All luggage must be checked in before departure.)
Han tok med seg *all* bagasj*en* på rommet. (He took all the luggage with him to his room.)
All mat smaker ikke like godt. (Not all food tastes equally good.)
Han måtte spise opp *all* mat*en*. (He had to eat up all the food.)

Alle dører stenges klokken 22.00. (All doors are closed at 10 p.m.)
Alle dørene i huset var stengt. (All the doors in the house were closed.)

d. «All», «alt» and «hele» must not be confused with each other:
hele brødet (the whole loaf, all the loaf)
alt brødet (all the bread; e.g. in the house)
alle brødene (all the loaves)

«Hele» is used to refer to a whole.
Examples:
hele brødet (the whole loaf, all the loaf)
hele verden (the whole world, all the world)
hele dagen (the whole day, all the day, all day)
hele folket (the whole nation, all the nation)
hele tiden (all the time, the whole time)

Wrong: Hun snakker all den tid

The correct form is: Hun snakker *hele* tiden. (She talks all the time.)

Wrong: Jeg arbeider all dagen

The correct form is: Jeg arbeider *hele* dagen. (I work all day.)

Remember that the definite article very rarely precedes «hele», but that the noun is in the definite form.

e. Special idioms:
I all verden, hva er dette? (Good heavens, what's this?)
I alle dager, hva skal dette bety? (What on earth does this mean?)

Note that «alt» can also be used in the same sense as «allerede» (already):
Han har *alt* kommet. / Han har kommet *alt*. (He has already come.)
De har *alt* gjort det. / De har gjort det *alt*. (They have already done it.)

HVER, HVERT

(each, every)

«Hver» and «enhver» precede masculine and feminine nouns,
«hvert» and «ethvert» are the neuter forms.

a. **Before a singular noun.**

Examples:

Hver dag går hun på skolen. (Every day she goes to school.)
Hvert år reiser hun hjem. (Every year she travels home.)

Note that the noun is always in the indefinite form following
«hver», «hvert», etc.

Wrong: Hver dagen, Hvert huset

The correct forms are:

Hver dag (Every day)
Hvert hus (Every house)

b. **Standing alone.**

Examples:

Bare én kake til *hver!* (Only one cake each / per person!)
De fikk en kake *hver.* (They each got a cake.)

ENHVER, ETHVERT

(each one, every one)

Enhver oppgave har sin verdi. (Every task has its value.)
Denne oppgaven er viktig for *enhver.* (This task is important for
each and every one.)

«Enhver», «ethvert» occur most frequently in certain idioms:

Enhver feie for sin egen dør! (Put your own house in order!)
Enhver gjøre sitt beste! (Everyone should do his best!)
Enhver sørge for seg selv! (Every man for himself!)
Ethvert hus må ha innlagt vann. (Every house must have water on
tap.)
Ethvert ønske kan ikke oppfylles. (Not every wish can come true.)

«Ethvert» occurs rarely on its own.
«Hver», «enhver» and «hvert», «ethvert» are very similar in meaning,
the difference tending to be one of degree. «Enhver», «ethvert»
emphasize the fact that we are talking about every single one.

131

ANNENHVER, ANNETHVERT

(= hver annen, hvert annet) (every other)

Hun gikk på skolen *annenhver* dag. (She went to school every other day; e.g. Monday, Wednesday and Friday.)

Annethvert år er det valg her. (Every other year there is an election here.)

With all other ordinal numbers, «hver» must come first:

Flyet går *hver* tredje time. (The plane goes every three hours.)

Ny president velges *hvert* fjerde år. (A new president is elected every four years.)

HVER VÅR, HVER SIN

(each . . . own)

In sentences with «hver» (each), the possessive pronoun is placed between «hver» and the noun.

De tok hver(t) *sitt* eple. (They each took their own apple; they took an apple each.)

Vi gikk hver *sin/vår* vei. (We each went our own way; we went our separate ways.)

«Vi gikk hver *sin* vei» is considered the most grammatically correct form, as «sin» refers back to «hver». Imagine the alternative sentence construction:

Hver (av oss) gikk *sin* vei. (Each one (of us) went his own way.)

However, «Vi gikk hver *vår* vei» is also commonly accepted as standard usage.

Note that *sin/sitt* agrees in number and gender with the noun to which it refers (*sitt* eple, *sin* vei).

Impersonal pronoun

DET

In addition to its other uses, «det» also functions as an impersonal pronoun.

a. **In impersonal sentences:**

Examples:

Det regner. (It is raining.)

Det er kaldt i Norge om vinteren. (It is cold in Norway in the winter.)

Det fortelles at Ibsen ofte gikk på restaurant. (It is said that Ibsen often went to restaurants.)
Hvordan har du *det?* (How are you?)
Det står bra til med meg. (I'm very well.)
Ha *det* (bra)! (Good bye!)

b. **When an indefinite noun is the subject of a sentence it is very common, to use the following construction, where the main verb is preceded by «det» and the subject comes afterwards.**
This construction corresponds closely to the English construction with «There is/are».
Examples:

Mange mennesker bor i Norge.→ *Det* bor mange mennesker i Norge.
(Many people live in Norway.) (There are many people living in Norway.)

En gutt står utenfor. → *Det* står en gutt utenfor.
(A boy is standing outside.) (There is a boy standing outside.)

Noen epler ligger på bordet. → *Det* ligger noen epler på bordet.
(Some apples are lying on the table.) (There are some apples on the table.)

c. **«Det» is used as the subject of sentences referring to time:**
Examples:
Det er mandag i dag. / I dag er *det* mandag.
(It's Monday today. / Today is Monday.)

Wrong: I dag er mandag.

Det var en gang en prins . . . / En gang var *det* en prins.
(Once upon a time there was a prince.)

Wrong: En gang var en prins . . .

Det er barneår i år. / I år er *det* barneår.
(It's the year of the child this year.)

Wrong: I år er barneår.

d. **As the subject of cleft sentences:**
   Examples:
   Han kommer. (He is coming.)
   Det er han som kommer. (It is he who is coming.)
   See the section on Relative pronouns.

CONJUNCTIONS

There are two types of conjunctions:

1. Coordinating conjunctions

- *og* (and), *både – og* (both – and)
- *men* (but)
- *for* (for)
- *eller* (or), *enten – eller* (either – or), *verken – eller* (neither – nor)

These conjunctions connect words, phrases, clauses and sentences (with the exception of «for», which can only connect whole sentences).
Examples:
Du *og* jeg. (You and I.)
Både du *og* jeg *og* Per *og* Anne. (You and me and Per and Anne.)
Han er norsk, *men* jeg er fransk. (He is Norwegian but I am French.)
Han kunne ikke hjelpe meg, *for* han hadde ikke tid. (He couldn't help me, for he didn't have time.)
Han kommer på fredag *eller* lørdag. (He is coming on Friday or Saturday.)

When the above conjunctions join together entire clauses, they must be the same *kinds* of clause; ie. two main clauses or two subordinate clauses.

There is no inversion of the subject and verb phrase in a clause introduced by a coordinating conjunction.
Example:
I dag er det kaldt, *men* det er pent vær. (Today it's cold but sunny.)

Wrong: I dag er det kaldt, men er det pent vær.

2. Subordinating conjunctions

Subordinating conjunctions always introduce a subordinate clause and will affect the word order of the clause (see part IV). The many different subordinating conjunctions can be divided into groups according to their meaning:

	at (that), om (if, whether)
Conjunctions of time:	da (when), når (whenever), før (before)
Conjunctions of cause:	fordi (because), ettersom (since)
Conjunctions of condition:	dersom (in case), hvis (if)
Conjunctions of concession:	til tross for at (in spite of), selv om (even if)
Conjunctions of purpose:	for at (in order that), så (at) (so)
Conjunctions of result:	så at (so that), slik at (such that), så (so)
Conjunctions of comparison:	som (as), slik som (like)

AT
(that) can often be omitted.
Examples:
Han sa *(at)* han ikke kunne komme. (He said (that) he couldn't come.)
Jeg tror *(at)* han er hjemme. (I think he's at home.)
Hun syntes *(at)* det var dyrt her. (She thought it was expensive here.)

However, «at» is obligatory in the following cases:
– when the subordinate clause comes first:
  At han kommer, er sikkert. (It is definite that he's coming.)

– following a preposition:
  De pekte *på at* det ikke var helt riktig. (They pointed out that it wasn't quite right.)

– after «enn»:
  Det er bedre (at) du går nå *enn at* du venter til i morgen. (It's better that you go now rather than waiting until tomorrow.)

- **when preceded by an intensifying adverbial phrase:**
  Han glemte *helt at* han skulle til legen. (He quite forgot that he was going to the doctor.)

- **when the word order of the subordinate clause does not follow the normal pattern, as is common in the case of indirect speech:**
  De sa *at* nå var det ikke kaldt ute. (They said that it wasn't cold outside now.)

Here, the subordinate clause has retained the word order of the original statement: «Nå er det ikke kaldt ute.» Otherwise, the sentence would be: «Da sa (at) det ikke var kaldt ute nå», which is equally correct.

OM
(if, whether)
Examples:
Jeg lurer på *om* han kommer. (I wonder if he is coming.)

Wrong: Jeg lurer på hvis han kommer

Han undret seg på *om* han kunne klare det. (He wondered if he could manage it.)
Jeg vet ikke *om* de kommer eller ikke. (I don't know whether they're coming or not.)

Wrong: Jeg vet ikke hvis de kommer eller ikke.

Wrong: Jeg vet ikke at de kommer eller ikke.

The verb *vite* (know) is almost always followed by *om*.
Han spurte *om* jeg ville komme. (He asked if I wanted to come.)

Wrong: Han spurte hvis jeg ville komme.

A general rule is that whenever «if» can be replaced by «whether», «om» is the correct conjunction.

CONJUNCTIONS OF TIME

da (when)   med det samme (as)
når (whenever)   fra (from when)
mens (while)   til, inntil (until)
før (before)   hver gang (every time)
idet (as)   etter hvert som (as)
etter at (after)   så lenge [som] (as long as)
siden (since)   så ofte [som] (as often as)
innen (before)   så snart [som] (as soon as)

Examples:
Mens det regnet, satt jeg inne. (While it rained I sat indoors.)
Han gikk *før* jeg fikk takket ham. (He left before I was able to thank him.)

Da, når
(when)
The general rule is that «når» is used for an action or event that is repeated, while «da» is used about a one-time occurrence, usually in the past. In addition, «når» is always used when referring to the future and in questions.
Examples:
Da jeg var liten, bodde jeg i India. (When I was little I lived in India.)
Når jeg blir gammel, skal jeg reise tilbake til India. (When I get old I shall go back to India.)
Når jeg besøkte dem, hadde jeg alltid med meg blomster. (When I visited them I always took flowers with me.)
Når var du der? *Da* jeg var liten. (When were you there? When I was little.)
Når skal du dit? *Når* jeg blir gammel. (When are you going there? When I get old.)

«Da» and «når» can also function as conjunctions of cause when they mean «as», «because».
Example:
Nå *da* det er så glatte veier, må vi bruke vinterdekk. (Because the roads are so slippery now, we must use winter tyres.)

138

Etter at, etter, etterpå
(after, afterwards)

Etter at (after):	conjunction
Etter (after):	preposition
Etterpå (afterwards):	adverb

Examples:
Etter at vi hadde spist, gikk vi en tur. (After we had eaten we went for a walk.)
Etter turen gikk vi hjem. (After the walk we went home.)
Etterpå så vi på fjernsyn. (Afterwards we watched television.)

Før, foran, tidligere
(before)
«Før» can be a preposition, a conjunction or an adverb.
a. When «før» is used as a preposition it can sometimes be replaced by «foran»; however, «foran» as a rule has to do with places, whereas «før» relates to time.
Examples:
Før/foran finalen var han veldig nervøs. (Before the final he was very nervous.)

Wrong: Foran ferien var han syk.

The correct form is: *Før* ferien var han syk. (Before the holiday he was ill.)

b. «Før» used as a conjunction cannot be replaced by «foran»:
Jeg spiste mye poteter *før* jeg kom til Norge. (I ate a lot of potatoes before I came to Norway.)

Wrong: Jeg spiste mye poteter foran jeg kom . . .

c. When «før» is used as an adverb it cannot be replaced by «foran», but instead by «tidligere» in many instances:
Jeg har hørt det *før/tidligere*. (I have heard that before/earlier.)

Certain fixed idioms always require «før»:
Før eller senere lærer du nok norsk! (Sooner or later you'll manage to learn Norwegian!)

Wrong: Tidligere eller senere lærer . . .

CONJUNCTIONS OF CAUSE

fordi (because)   siden (since)   ettersom (as)

da (as)   når (if, as)

Examples:

Hun gjorde det *fordi* hun hadde lyst til det. (She did it because she wanted to.)

Når/Da/Siden/Ettersom det ikke passer for dem, må vi finne en annen dag. (Since/As it doesn't suit them, we'll have to find another day.)

Fordi, for

(because)

The coordinating conjunction «for» means the same as «fordi», but can only connect two main clauses.

Examples:

Han kan ikke komme *for* han har ikke tid. (He can't come because he doesn't have time.)

Han kan ikke komme *fordi* han ikke har tid. (He can't come because he doesn't have time.)

Fordi, derfor

(because, therefore)

Examples:

Han kan ikke komme. (He can't come.)

Hvorfor kan han ikke komme? (Why can't he come?)

Fordi han er syk. (Because he's ill.)

Han er syk, *derfor* kan han ikke komme. (He's ill, therefore/so he can't come.)

Han leser norsk. (He is studying Norwegian.)

Hvorfor leser han norsk? (Why is he studying Norwegian?)

Fordi han bor i Norge. (Because he lives in Norway.)

Han bor i Norge, *derfor* leser han norsk. (He lives in Norway, so he is studying Norwegian.)

Wrong: Hvorfor leser du norsk? Derfor jeg bor i Norge.

The correct form is: *Fordi* jeg bor i Norge . . . (Because I live in Norway . . .)

«Derfor» can never be used to answer a question beginning with «Hvorfor».

CONJUNCTIONS OF CONDITION

dersom (if, in case)
hvis (ikke) (if (not))
så fremt (provided that)
så sant (provided)
om (if)
når (if)

i fall, i tilfelle (in case)
med mindre (unless)
uten at (without)
bare (if only, as long as)
for så vidt som (in so far as)

Examples:
Om/Hvis du vil, kan jeg hjelpe deg. (If you want I can help you.)
I fall / I tilfelle han kommer, må du fortelle ham det. (If he comes you must tell him that.)
Jeg skal gjøre det *så sant* jeg kan. (I shall do it if I can.)
Vi har nok også skyld i dette *for så vidt som* vi ikke gjorde noe for å forhindre det. (Well, we are also to blame in so far as we didn't do anything to prevent it.)

Jeg skal gjøre det
{
så sant jeg får tid.
hvis jeg bare får tid.
bare jeg får tid til det.
}
(I shall do it if I have time.)

Vi kommer
{
med mindre det kommer noe i veien.
hvis det *ikke* kommer noe i veien.
dersom det *ikke* kommer noe i veien.
så sant det *ikke* kommer noe i veien.
så fremt det *ikke* kommer noe i veien.
bare det *ikke* kommer noe i veien.
}

(We are coming,
{
provided nothing
as long as nothing
unless something
}
gets in the way.)

A condition can also be expressed without any conjunction at all, simply by inverting the word order; ie. the verb is placed before the subject.
Examples:
Hvis han kommer, går jeg.
Kommer han, (så) går jeg.
} (If he comes, I'm going.)

141

I tilfelle det blir regn, blir vi hjemme.
Blir det regn, (så) blir vi hjemme. } (If it rains we'll stay at home.)

Uten at, uten å

(without, unless)

One can choose between a construction with or without the infinitive to express *without* in a conditional clause provided that the subject in the main clause is identical with that in the subordinate clause.

Examples:

De så på slåsskampen { *uten* å løfte en finger.
{ *uten at* de løftet en finger.

(They watched the fight without lifting a finger.)

ie. the subject («de») is the same in both clauses.

Han falt og slo seg { *uten* å felle en tåre.
{ *uten at* han felte en tåre.

(He fell and hurt himself without shedding a tear.)

Again, «han» is the subject of both clauses.

However, when there are different subjects, the construction with «uten at» is obligatory:

Examples:

Drømmen kunne ikke oppfylles *uten at* han reiste til Norge. (The dream could not come true unless he went to Norway.)

Wrong: Drømmen kunne ikke oppfylles uten å reise . . .

Here there are two different subjects: first «drømmen», then «han».

Men dette kunne realiseres *uten at* elevene konkurrerte med hverandre. (But this could be implemented without the pupils competing with each other.)

The two subjects in this sentence are «dette» and «elevene».

CONJUNCTIONS OF CONCESSION

enda (although)	fordi om (owing to the fact that)
skjønt (although)	enda om (even though)

om (if)	selv om (even though)
om enn (even if)	hva enn (regardless of what)
hva så (whatever)	til tross for at (in spite of the fact that)
trass i at (despite)	hvor enn (regardless of where)
hvor så (however)	uansett (regardless of)
samme (regardless of)	

Examples:

Trass i at
Til tross for at } det regnet, jogget han.

(In spite of the fact that it was raining, he went jogging.)

Skjønt
Selv om } det regnet, jogget han.

(Although/even though it was raining, he went jogging.)
Enda han ikke var norsk, snakket han norsk. (Although he wasn't Norwegian, he spoke Norwegian.)
Selv om du gav meg 100 kroner, ville jeg ikke si det. (Even if you gave me a hundred kroner, I wouldn't say it.)

Jeg skal ha den {
om det *så*
selv om det
samme om det
uansett om det
} skal koste meg livet.

(I shall have it, even if it costs me my life.)

Huset ville han ha *hvor* dyrt det *så/enn* skulle bli. (He wanted the house, however expensive it might be.)
Jeg skal delta *hva som enn* skjer. (I shall take part whatever happens.)
Jeg skal gå *uansett* hvor langt det er. (I'm going to walk, regardless of how far it is.)

CONJUNCTIONS OF PURPOSE
For at, så (at)
(so that, so)
Examples:
Han tok på seg varme klær *så (at)* han ikke skulle bli syk. (He put on warm clothes so that he wouldn't become ill.)
Snekkeren arbeidet dag og natt *for at* huset skulle bli ferdig til jul. (The carpenter worked day and night so that the house would be ready by Christmas.)

Han gjemte seg i kjelleren *for at* de ikke skulle finne ham. (He hid in the basement so that they wouldn't find him.)

An alternative construction in a clause introduced by a conjunction of purpose is «for» + («ikke») + infinitive. In this case, the subject of the subordinate clause must be identical to the subject of the main clause.
Examples:
Han gjemte seg *for ikke å bli* funnet. (He hid so as not to be found.)
Han arbeidet *for å få* huset ferdig. (He worked hard so as to get the house finished.)
Han kledde seg godt *for ikke å bli* syk. (He dressed up warmly so as not to become ill.)

CONJUNCTIONS OF RESULT

Så at (so)	slik at (such that)
så (so)	sånn at (such that)

Examples:
Han var *så* syk *at* han ikke kunne komme. (He was so ill that he couldn't come.)
De bråkte *så* jeg ikke fikk sove. (They made so much noise that I couldn't get to sleep.)

«Så» can have the following functions:
1. **As a conjunction of result:**
   De bråkte { *så* jeg ikke fikk sove.
   { *slik at* jeg ikke fikk sove.
   (They made so much noise that I couldn't get to sleep.)

2. **As a conjunction of purpose:**
   De bråkte *så* jeg ikke skulle få sove. (They made a lot of noise so that I wouldn't get to sleep.)

3. **Coordinating conjunction, meaning «because of which»:**
   De bråkte så jeg fikk ikke sove. (They made a lot of noise, so I couldn't get to sleep.)

4. **As an adverb:**
   Først skulle han komme, *så* skulle han ikke komme. (First he was going to come, then he wasn't going to come.)

144

CONJUNCTIONS OF COMPARISON

som (as)   enn (than)
slik som (like)   dess . . . dess (the . . . the)
så som (such as)   jo . . . dess (the . . . the)
som om (as if)   jo . . . desto (the . . . the)

Examples:

Som man sår, høster man. (As a man sows, so shall he reap.)
Det gikk *så som* / *slik som* jeg sa. (It went like I said.)
Han snakket *som om* han eide hele verden. (He talked as if he owned the whole world.)
Jo/dess mer du spiser, *desto/dess/jo* tykkere blir du. (The more you eat, the fatter you'll get.)
Note the word order here in the subordinate clause!

When the subject is compared with itself, «som» is usually dropped.
Examples:
De gjør så godt (som) de kan. (They do the best they can.)
Han kom så fort (som) han kunne. (He came as fast as he could.)

But: Han kom så fort *som* lynet. (He came as quick as a flash.)

INTERJECTIONS

Interjections are purely emotive responses which express feelings, emotions and sensations such as pain, joy, contempt, anger, etc.
Examples:

fy (shame)	hei (hi, hello)	fillern (damn, bother)
au (ouch)	takk (thank you)	åh (oh)
æsj (ugh)	hm (mm)	isj (phooey)
hurra (hurray)	fanden (damn)	hallo (here!, hey, hello)
uff (oh dear)	pokker (blast, bother)	

The negative and affirmative responses also belong in this category:
ja, jo (yes)
nei (no)

Ja, jo
«Ja» is the correct response to a positive question, «jo» to a negative question:
Examples:
Snakker du norsk? *Ja.* (Do you speak Norwegian? Yes.)
Snakker du ikke norsk? *Jo.* (Don't you speak Norwegian? Yes.)

The responses «nei» and «ja» can also be used in certain contexts without functioning as a direct negative or affirmative, in which case they often serve the purpose of giving emphasis and spontaneity to an utterance:
Examples:
Nei, så fin du er nå. (Gosh, how nice you look now.)
Det går bra, *ja.* (It's going well, indeed.)
Hele tida, *ja* hvert minutt, maste de på henne. (The whole time, every minute in fact, they were nagging her.)

146

NUMERALS

Cardinals   ## Ordinals

	Cardinals		Ordinals	
0	null	(zero, nought)	(nullte)	–
1	en/ett/ene	(one)	første	(first)
2	to	(two)	annen/annet/andre	(second)
3	tre	(three)	tredje	(third)
4	fire	(four)	fjerde	(fourth)
5	fem	(five)	femte	(fifth)
6	seks	(six)	sjette	(sixth)
7	sju/syv	(seven)	sjuende/syvende	(seventh)
8	åtte	(eight)	åttende	(eighth)
9	ni	(nine)	niende	(ninth)
10	ti	(ten)	tiende	(tenth)
11	elleve	(eleven)	ellevte	(eleventh)
12	tolv	(twelve)	tolvte	(twelfth)
13	tretten	(thirteen)	trettende	(thirteenth)
14	fjorten	(fourteen)	fjortende	(fourteenth)
15	femten	(fifteen)	femtende	(fifteenth)
16	seksten	(sixteen)	sekstende	(sixteenth)
17	sytten	(seventeen)	syttende	(seventeenth)
18	atten	(eighteen)	attende	(eighteenth)
19	nitten	(nineteen)	nittende	(nineteenth)
20	tjue/tyve	(twenty)	tjuende/tyvende	(twentieth)
21	tjueen/enogtyve	(twenty-one)	tjueførste/enogtyvende	(twenty-first)
30	tretti/tredve	(thirty)	trettiende/tredevte	(thirtieth)
40	førti (førr)	(forty)	førtiende	(fortieth)
50	femti	(fifty)	femtiende	(fiftieth)
60	seksti	(sixty)	sekstiende	(sixtieth)
70	sytti	(seventy)	syttiende	(seventieth)
80	åtti	(eighty)	åttiende	(eightieth)
90	nitti	(ninety)	nittiende	(ninetieth)
100	hundre	(hundred)	hundrede	(hundredth)
101	(ett)hundreogen	(hundred and one)	hundreogførste	(hundred and first)
169	(ett)hundreog-sekstini/ hundreogniogseksti	(hundred and sixty nine)	hundreogsekstiniende/ hundreogniog-sekstiende	(hundred and sixty ninth)
200	tohundre	(two hundred)	tohundrede	(two hundredth)
1000	(ett) tusen	(thousand)	tusende	(thousandth)
1001	(ett) tusenogen	(one thousand and one)	tusenogførste	(thousandth and first)
2001	totusenogen	(two thousand and one)	totusenogførste	(two thousandth and first)
	en million	(one million)	millionte	(millionth)
	to millioner	(two million)		
	en milliard	(one billion)		

Note that all compound numerals in Norwegian are written as one word, including «og» (and) when applicable.

In Norwegian two ways of expressing compound numerals are used. Either the English pattern is followed (*trettini* (39), *sekstifire* (64) and so on), or the last number is put first and linked with «og» (and): e.g. *treogførti* (43), literally three-and-forty).

EN, ÉN/ET, ETT

«én» (before masculine or feminine nouns) and «ett» (before neuter nouns) are used to indicate «one» as opposed to *«a»/«an»*.
Examples:
Jeg vil bare ha én kake. (I only want one cake.)
Jeg skal bo her bare ett år. (I shall only live here for one year.)

EN, ETT

«En» (one) does not inflect when it is part of a compound numeral or when part of a decimal figure.
Examples:

	Read
1 år	*ett* år (one year)
21 år	tjue*en* år (twenty-one years)
1 eple	*ett* eple (one apple)
31 epler	tretti*en* epler (thirty-one apples)
1 poeng	*ett* poeng (one point)
0,1 poeng	null komma *en* poeng (nought point one point)
1 g	*ett* gram (one gramme)
2,1 g	to komma *en* gram (two point one grammes)
kl 0100	klokka er *ett* (It's one a.m.)
kl 0101	klokka er *ett* minutt over *ett* (It's one minute past one a.m.)

Hun er nummer *én* i klassen. (She is number one in the class.)
De bor i hus nummer *én*. (They live in house number one.)

ett kapittel (one chapter)
ett vers (one verse)

But note: I kapittel *én*, vers *én*, står det . . . (In chapter one, verse one, it states . . .)

ANNEN, ANNET, ANDRE
(second)
See the chapters on the Indefinite pronouns and Adjectives.

ALTERNATIVE FORMS

Some of the cardinal numbers have two forms, for example «sju», «syv» (7), «tjue», «tyve» (20), «tretti», «tredve» (30). Both forms are commonly used, but the last form in each pair is the more conservative. The choice is free, but one should be consistent; ie. stick to «tyve» if you normally use «syv», but use «tjue» if «sju» falls more naturally.

Remember that in compounds one must *either* use the more conservative form with the linking «og», *or* the other form without linking «og».
Examples:

syvogtyve
tjuesju $\Big\}$ 27

DATES and AGE

I dag er det 1. november 1979. / 1.11.1979.
  Read: «første november nittensyttini / første i ellevte nittensyttini (or nittenniogsytti)»
(Today is the first of November, nineteen seventy-nine)

Han er født 6. februar 1967.
  Read: «sjette februar nittensekstisju (or nittensyvogseksti)»
(He was born on the sixth of February nineteen sixty-seven.)

på attenhundretallet
på 1800-tallet $\Big\}$ (in the eighteen hundreds)
i det nittende århundre
i det 19. århundre $\Big\}$ (in the nineteenth century)

i trettiårene:
1. in the thirties (ie. 1930–1939)
2. in her/his/their thirties, referring to a person's age.

i slutten av trettiårene / 30-årene (at the end of the/his/
sist i trettiårene / 30-årene   her/their thirties)

i de siste tretti årene / 30 årene (in the past 30 years)
i de neste tretti årene / 30 årene (in the next 30 years)

en tiåring
en 10-åring $\Big\}$ (a ten-year-old)

10 år gammel   (ten years old)

i tiårsalderen
i 10-årsalderen $\Big\}$ (about 10 years old)

et tiår (a decade)
De har vært her i årtier. (They have been here for decades.)

FRACTIONS

1/2:   en halvdel (one half)
      en halv agurk / halvparten av agurken (half a cucumber,
      a half cucumber)
      et halvt eple (half an apple)
2/2:   to halve (two halves)

1/3:   en tredel /tredjedel (one third)
2/3:   to tredeler/tredjedeler (two thirds)
1/4:   en firedel/fjerdedel / kvart (one fourth/quarter)
1/13:   en trettendedel (one thirteenth)
1/14:   en fjortendedel (one fourteenth), etc.
1/1000:   en promille (one thousandth)
      en tusendel

1 1/2:   halvannen / en og en halv (one and a half)
      halvannen dag (one and a half days / a day and a half)
      halvannet eple (one and a half apples / an apple and a half)

7 timer (7 hours)
7 1/2 *time* (7 and a half hours)
Note that the noun is in the singular following a fraction.

Note also the following paradigm:
7 °C   Read: sju grader (Celsius) (seven degrees Celsius)
7 1/2 °C Read: sju og en halv *grad* (seven and a half degrees)
7,5 °C   Read: sju komma fem grad*er* (seven point five degrees)

THE CLOCK

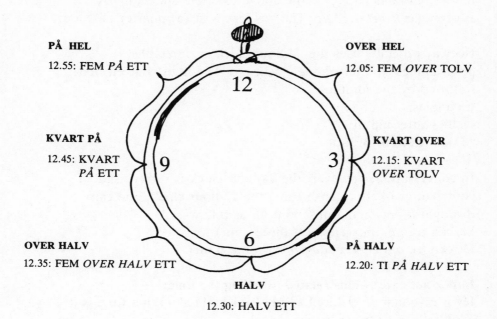

PÅ HEL
12.55: FEM *PÅ* ETT

OVER HEL
12.05: FEM *OVER* TOLV

KVART PÅ
12.45: KVART *PÅ* ETT

KVART OVER
12.15: KVART *OVER* TOLV

OVER HALV
12.35: FEM *OVER HALV* ETT

PÅ HALV
12.20: TI *PÅ HALV* ETT

HALV
12.30: HALV ETT

For the purpose of telling the time, Norwegian divides the clock into quarters. For the first quarter after the hour, the number of minutes past («over») the hour is used; for the second quarter, one refers to the number of minutes *before* («på») the *half-hour*; for the third quarter, the number of minutes past («over») the *half-hour*; and for the last quarter, the minutes before («på») the hour. The examples in the diagram illustrate the system.

Note especially that, when referring to the half-hour, Norwegian uses the *next* hour, whereas English uses the *previous* hour. Thus «halv ti» is *not* the same as its direct translation into colloquial English, half ten (10.30), but means *nine thirty* (9.30). It can often be easier to think in terms of «half *to* ten» etc. to avoid confusion.

As the examples show, Norwegian usually omits «minutter» (minutes) when telling the time. This is the same in English for expressions with five and its multiples (five past eight, twenty to nine, etc.), but Norwegian also leaves out «minutes» for other numbers. Example:
Neste trikk går *syv på halv*. (The next tram goes at 23 minutes past.)

151

It is important to remember that, when telling the time, Norwegian never translates «at». See the above example and similarly:
Bussen går *kvart over ti*. (The bus leaves at (a) quarter past ten.)

Norway officially uses the 24-hour clock in timetables, programmes, the telephone clock, etc. The hour is given first, followed by the minutes.
Examples:
08.09 – åtte null ni
13.48 – tretten førtiåtte

In conversation, however, the 24-hour clock is rarely used. If confusion is likely to arise using the 12-hour clock, one can distinguish between a.m. and p.m. as follows:
klokka tre *om morgenen* (at three a.m.)
klokka tre *om ettermiddagen* (at three p.m.)

Important expressions related to telling the time:
Hvor mye/mange er klokka? / Hva er klokka? (What time is it?)
Klokka/Den er to. (It's two o'clock.)

Wrong: Det er klokka to.

Note: Klokka *ett* (One o'clock)

Wrong: Klokka en

Jeg kommer *klokka fem presis*. (I'll be there at five o'clock sharp.)
Klokka er *akkurat elleve*. (It's exactly eleven o'clock.)
Når kommer du? – Jeg kommer mandag. (When are you coming? – I'm coming on Monday.)
Hvilket klokkeslett kommer du? – Jeg kommer klokka fem. (What time are you coming? – I'm coming at five o'clock.)

Cirka klokka åtte ⎫
Ved åtte-tiden ⎬ (at about eight o'clock)
Rundt åtte ⎭

Jeg kjører vanligvis til byen *på ett kvarter / en halv time / tre kvarter*. (It usually takes me a quarter of an hour / half an hour / three quarters of an hour to drive to town.)

Du kan gå til toppen av fjellet *på fem kvarter*. (You can walk to the top of the mountain in an hour and a quarter.)

(In this last example it is also possible to say «. . . på en time og et kvarter.»)

Det tar en *drøy* time å kjøre til mine foreldre. (It takes just over an hour to drive to my parents.)
Hun brukte en *snau* time på oppgaven. (She spent just under an hour on the exercise.)

MONEY

Kr 3,–   Read: tre kroner / kroner tre (three kroner)
Kr 3,50   Read: tre kroner og femti øre / tre femti / tre og en halv
          krone (three kroner and fifty øre /three fifty / three and
          a half kroner)
Kr 1,50   Read: en krone og femti øre / kroner én femti /
          halvannen krone (one krone and fifty øre / one fifty / one
          and a half kroner)
Kr 51,–   Read: kroner femtien / en og femti kroner
          (fifty-one kroner)

The Norwegian coins and notes are referred to as:

en tiøring (ten-øre coin)
en femtiøring (fifty-øre coin)
en krone / et kronestykke (one-krone coin) = 100 øre
en femmer / femkrone / femkroning (five-kroner coin)
en tier (ten-kroner coin – formerly: en tikroneseddel (ten-kroner note))
en femtilapp / femtikroneseddel (fifty-kroner note)
en hundrelapp / hundrekroneseddel (hundred-kroner note)
en tusenlapp / tusenkroneseddel (thousand-kroner note)

SOME IDIOMS

Nå er *hundre og ett* ute. (Now the fat is in the fire.)
Tusen takk. (Thanks very much, many thanks.)
Jeg har *tusen* ting å gjøre i dag. (I've got a hundred and one things to do today.)
I dag har det gått i *ett* kjør. (The whole day has been a whirl.)
Han fikk en *tolver* i tipping. (He got 12 right in the football pools.)

Hun er en *ener*. (She is in a class of her own.)
Jeg skal være her *en fem–seks* år. (I shall be here about 5 to 6 years.)
Han bor i *fireren*. (He lives in house/block number four.)

NUMERALS WRITTEN AS WORDS OR FIGURES

1. **Figures are normally used:**
   a. **for money, weights and measures.**
   Examples:
   Det kostet til sammen *20* kroner. (It cost 20 kroner altogether.)
   Veien var *60* km lang. (The road was 60 kilometres long.)
   Hun kjøpte *2* hg salami. (She bought 2 hectogrammes of salami.)

   Examples with numerals in this category expressed in words can sometimes be found, however:
   Jeg fikk *fem* kroner av onkelen min. (I was given five kroner by my uncle.)

   b. **for large numbers.**
   Examples:
   Året har *365* dager. (There are 365 days in a year.)
   But note: Jeg var der i *fjorten* dager. (I was there for a fortnight, ie. fourteen days.)

   c. **for dates** – see the section on Dates and Age.

2. **Words are more common:**
   a. **with small numbers.**
   Examples:
   Hun kjøpte *fire* roser. (She bought four roses.)
   Vi reiste alle *fire*. (All four of us went.)
   Jeg har *to* brødre. (I have two brothers.)

   b. **in compounds such as the following:**
   *tre*kant (triangle)
   *fem*øring (five-øre coin)
   *tre*delt (divided in three)
   *fire*sifret (four-figure), etc.

c. **when an ordinal number is used adjectivally.**
   Examples:
   Den *første* dagen i uka. (The first day of the week.)
   Den *fjerde* gutten var norsk. (The fourth boy was
   Norwegian.)
   But note: Han er født 5. mars 1967. (He was born on March
   5th, 1967.)

3. **In various other expressions containing numerals, the choice of words or figures is optional.**
   3-årsalderen/treårsalderen (the age of 3)
   3-åring/treåring (three-year-old)
   10-årsjubileum/tiårsjubileum (tenth anniversary)

PREPOSITIONS

for (for)	etter (after)	ved (at)
til (to)	av (of, by)	med (with)
fra (from)	om (about)	mellom (between)
over (over)	på (at, on)	mot (against)
før (before)	hos (with)	blant (among)
under (under)	i (in)	etc.

It is impossible to give hard and fast rules for the use of a particular preposition. The only solution is to learn the prepositional phrases as they occur and in context. However, the following points give some general guidelines.

PREPOSITIONS RELATED TO PLACE
A. **Distinguishing between being «at» a place and movement «to» a place.**
   Examples:
   Jeg bor *på* Blindern. (I live at Blindern [the Oslo university campus].)
   Jeg går *til* Blindern. (I walk to Blindern.)
   Jeg bor *i* Bergen. (I live in Bergen.)
   Jeg reiser *til* Bergen. (I travel to Bergen.)
   Hun arbeider *på* Toten. (She works in Toten.)
   Hun reiser *til* Toten. (She travels to Toten.)
   De er *i* Mandal. (They are in Mandal.)
   De reiser *til* Mandal. (They travel to Mandal.)
   Hun ferierer *på* Kanariøyene. (She is on holiday in the Canary Islands.)
   Hun reiste *til* Kanariøyene. (She travelled to the Canary Islands.)
   Hun studerer *i* England. (She is studying in England.)
   Hun drar *til* England. (She is going to England.)

The following guidelines may help in the choice of preposition in connection with the «stative» verbs (to be, live, etc.):
«På» is used for villages and small towns and for islands which are not independent countries;
«I» is used with names of countries and larger towns and also very often for towns and villages situated on the coast, regardless of size.

«Til» is used with «directional» verbs, such as to travel, go, come, etc.

Wrong: Jeg kom i Norge for to måneder siden.

The correct form is: Jeg kom *til* Norge for to måneder siden. (I came to Norway two months ago.)

«Til» is also found in idioms where the following noun takes the genitive -s (see the section on Genitives).
Examples:

til sjøs (to sea)	til fots (on foot)
til bords (to the table)	til fjells (to the mountains)
til sengs (to bed)	til skogs (to the woods)

In certain set phrases the same preposition is used both to refer to being *at* a place and motion *towards* a place.
Examples:
Hun er *på* jobb(en)/arbeid(et). (She is at work.)
Hun går *på* jobb(en)/arbeid(et). (She goes to work.)
Han er *på* kino. (He's at the cinema.)
Han går *på* kino. (He goes to the cinema.)
Han er *på* apoteket. (He's at the chemist's.)
Han skal *på* apoteket. (He's going to the chemist's.)
Han er *på* postkontoret. (He's at the post office.)
Han skal *på* postkontoret. (He's going to the post office.)
Hun er *på* kontoret. (She's at the office.)
Hun går *på* kontoret. (She's going to the office.)
De er *på* restaurant. (They are at a restaurant.)
De går ofte *på* restaurant. (They often go to a restaurant.)
Han er *på* badet/kjøkkenet. (He is in the bathroom/the kitchen.)
Han gikk *på* badet/kjøkkenet. (He went to the bathroom/the kitchen.)

Han er *på/i* butikken. (He's at/in the shop.)
Han skal *på/i* butikken. (He's going to the shop.)
De er *i* teater. (They are at the theatre.)
De går ofte *i* teater. (They often go to the theatre.)
Hun er *i* kirken. (She's at church.)
Hun går *i* kirken. (She goes to church.)
Hun er *i* banken. (She's at the bank.)
Hun går *i* banken. (She goes to the bank.)

Alternatively, the preposition «til» is also correct in most of these phrases with a directional verb, but then the meaning is usually altered to refer to the actual building, rather than its function. For example:
Hun går *til* kirken. (She goes to the church.)
This sentence indicates that she goes to the building that is the church, but not necessarily that she goes inside to a service.

B. **Prepositions denoting being at a place or movement towards a place wich involve people and professions:**
Examples:
Hun bor *hos* oss. (She lives with us.)
Hun kommer *til* oss. (She is coming to our house.)
Han er *hos* legen. (He is at the doctor's.)
Han går *til* legen. (He is going to the doctor's.)
De er *hos* kjøpmannen. (They are at the grocer's.)
De skal *til* kjøpmannen. (They are going to the grocer's.)
Hun sitter *hos* frisøren. (She is at the hairdresser's.)
Hun skal *til* frisøren. (She is going to the hairdresser's.)
Han er *hos* politiet. (He's with the police.)
Han skal *til* politiet. (He's going to the police.)
Papirene er *hos* myndighetene. (The papers are with the authorities.)
De er sendt *til* myndighetene. (They have been sent to the authorities.)

«Hos» is used for being at a place involving people, whereas «til» is used for motion towards that place.

Wrong: Vil du komme hos meg? Jeg skal gå på legen. Han er på legen.

PREPOSITIONS RELATED TO TIME
See the section on Adverbial phrases of time.

PREPOSITIONS RELATED TO PURPOSE
Examples:
Han kom *for å* hilse på henne. (He came to greet her.)
Hun reiste til byen *for å* handle. (She went to town to go shopping.)
De gikk *for å* se en film. (They went to see a film.)

«For å» reflects the underlying meaning «in order to». A useful guide to the correct use of «for å» is a test with «hvorfor» (why): if one can logically ask «why?» after the main verb, then «for å» is the correct continuation:
Han kom (hvorfor?) for å hilse på henne.
Hun reiste (hvorfor?) for å handle.

PREPOSITIONS RELATED TO MEANS
Examples:
Han spiste *med* skje og gaffel. (He ate with a spoon and fork.)
Han snekret *med* sag og hammer. (He did woodwork with a saw and hammer.)
Hun skrev *med* penn. (She wrote with a pen.)
De reiser *med* tog/båt/bil/buss, etc. (They travel by train/boat/car/bus, etc.)

PREPOSITIONS RELATED TO ATTRIBUTES
Examples:
Hvilken *størrelse* er det *på* skoene? (What size are the shoes?)
Hvilken *farge* er det *på* huset? (What colour is the house? / What is the colour of the house?)
Hvilket *nummer* er det *på* bussen? (What is the number of the bus?)
Hva er *prisen på* boka? (What is the price of the book?)
Hva er *tittelen på* boka? (What is the title of the book?)
Hva er *navnet på* barnet? (What is the name of the child? / What is the child's name?)

PREPOSITIONS REFLECTING THE GENITIVE
Examples:
Sønnen *til* broren min. (My brother's son.)
Mannen *til* søstera mi. (My sister's husband.)
Boka *til* Per. (Per's book.)

Note the difference between:

Hun kjøpte blomster *til* moren sin. (She bought flowers for her mother [as a gift].)

Hun kjøpte blomster *for* moren sin. (She bought flowers for her mother [on her mother's behalf].)

Note also:

Hun er en venn *av* meg. (She is a friend of mine.)

PREPOSITIONS IN THE PASSIVE TENSE

Examples:

Han skrev boka. Boka ble skrevet *av* ham. (He wrote the book. The book was written by him.)

En bok *av* Ibsen. (A book by Ibsen.)

Han eier huset. Huset eies *av* ham. (He owns the house. The house is owned by him.)

Han oppfant kruttet. Kruttet ble oppfunnet *av* ham. (He invented gunpowder. Gunpowder was invented by him.)

Han er oppfinneren *av* kruttet. (He is the inventor of gunpowder.)

PREPOSITIONAL PHRASES WHICH REPLACE GENITIVES

a. **Ownership/belonging:**

Pers sønn   →   sønnen *til* Per (Per's son)

guttens bok   →   boka *til* gutten (the boy's book)

b. **Part of a whole, usually corresponding to «of»:**

hundens hale → halen *på* hunden (the dog's tail)

husets tak → taket *på* huset (the house's roof)

treets grener → grenene *på* treet (the tree's branches)

c. **Within a specific area, usually corresponding to «in» or «of»:**

landets innbyggere → innbyggerne *i* landet (the country's inhabitants)

skogens trær → trærne *i* skogen (the trees in the forest)

landets hovedstad → hovedstaden *i* landet (the country's capital)

d. **Attributes, usually corresponding to «of»:**

husets farge → fargen *på* huset (the colour of the house)

husets størrelse → størrelsen *på* huset (the size of the house)

husets pris → prisen *på* huset (the price of the house)

husets nummer	→	nummeret *på* huset (the number of the house)
guttens navn	→	navnet *på* gutten (the name of the boy / the boy's name)
barnets alder	→	alderen *på* barnet (the age of the child / the child's age)

e. **«The person in charge» of a specific entity, usually corresponding to «of»:**

skipets kaptein	→	kapteinen *på* skipet (the ship's captain / the captain of the ship)
bussens sjåfør	→	sjåføren *på* bussen (the driver of the bus)
avdelingens lege	→	legen *på* avdelingen (the doctor on the ward)
Norges konge	→	kongen *i* Norge (the king of Norway)
Norges statsminister	→	statsministeren *i* Norge (Norway's prime minister / the prime minister of Norway)
komiteens formann	→	formannen *i* komiteen (the committee's chairman / the chairman of the committee)

f. **«The head» of a group of people or an institution:**

elevenes representant (elevrepresentant)	→	representanten *for* elevene (the pupils' representative)
orkesterets dirigent	→	dirigenten *for* orkesteret (the orchestra's conductor)
teatrets sjef (teatersjefen)	→	sjefen *for* teatret (the theatre manager)
personalets sjef (personalsjefen)	→	sjefen *for* personalet (the personnel manager)

PREPOSITIONAL PHRASES WHICH REPLACE COMPOUND NOUNS

en gullring (a gold ring)	→	en ring *av* gull (a ring (made) of gold)
et trehus (a wooden house)	→	et hus *av* tre (a house of wood)
en ullgenser (a woollen sweater)	→	en genser *av* ull (a sweater (made) of wool)
en porselenskopp (a china cup)	→	en kopp *av* porselen (a cup made of china)

161

Note the difference between these phrases and «en kopp te» (a cup of tea).

Wrong: en kopp av te
− a teacup is not made of tea!

IDIOMATIC PREPOSITIONAL PHRASES
The following list includes many frequently encountered prepositional phrases for each preposition.

Av
være avhengig av (be dependent on)
 Han er avhengig av sine foreldre. (He is dependent on his parents.)
leve av (live on)
 Han lever av frukt og grønnsaker. (He lives on fruit and vegetables.)
holde av (like)
 Han holder av henne. (He likes her.)
låne av (borrow from)
 Du kan få låne denne boka av meg. (You may borrow this book from me.)
slå av (turn off)
 Slå av motoren! (Turn off the engine!)
skru av (turn off)
 Skru av plata, er du snill! (Would you turn the hotplate off, please!)
gå av (get off, alight; retire)
 Du må gå av bussen ved Kirkeveien. (You must get off the bus at Church Street.)
 Han gikk av bussen. (He got off the bus.)
 Han har gått av med pensjon. (He has retired.)
ta av (take off; lose weight; clear; turn off; take care of)
 Ta av deg klærne! (Take off your clothes!)
 Flyet tok av for en time siden. (The plane took off an hour ago.)
 Hun har tatt av tre kilo på to uker. (She has lost three kilos in two weeks.)
 Ta av bordet, er du snill! (Would you clear the table, please!)
 Ta av til venstre første vei! (Turn off on the first road on the left!)

Jeg skal ta meg av den saken. (I'll take care of that matter.)

laget av (made of)

Fatet er laget av tre. (The dish is made of wood.)

bli lei av (get fed up with)

De ble lei av det dårlige været. (They got fed up with the bad weather.)

ha godt av (do someone good; serve someone right)

Hun har godt av litt ferie nå. (A holiday now will do her good.)

Det har du godt av! (It serves you right!)

ha vondt av (feel sorry for; have a hard time)

Jeg har vondt av dem. (I feel sorry for them.)

Han har vondt av de pengene jeg vant. (He has a hard time with the money I won.)

slappe av (take it easy)

Du kan slappe av etter eksamen. (You can take it easy after the exams.)

være medlem av (belong to, be a member of)

Hun er medlem av denne foreningen. (She belongs to this society.)

være opptatt av (be busy with, concerned about)

Hun er opptatt av disse problemene. (She is concerned about these problems.)

komme av (be due to)

Jeg vet ikke hva det kan komme av. (I don't know what that can be due to. / I don't know why that is.)

ha inntrykk av (have the impression)

Jeg har inntrykk av at de har mye penger. (I have the impression that they have a lot of money.)

Etter

høre etter (listen out for; listen carefully)

Kan du høre etter barna mens jeg er ute? (Can you listen out for the children while I'm out?)

Nå må du høre godt etter når jeg snakker til deg, for det er så viktig. (You must listen carefully when I talk to you, for it's very important.)

ta etter (copy; reach for)

Hun tar etter alt det gale han gjør. (She copies all the bad things he does.)

Han tok etter hånden hennes. (He reached for her hand.)

se etter (look for; look after)

Hva ser du etter? (What are you looking for?)

Kan du se etter barna mens vi er borte? (Can you look after the children while we are away?)

gå etter (examine; go by; go to get)

Han gikk alt nøye etter. (He examined everything carefully.)

Han gikk etter klokka. (He went by the clock.)

Han gikk etter posten. (He went to get the post.)

lete etter (look for)

Hva leter du etter? (What are you looking for?)

rette seg etter (conform to, abide by)

Du må rette deg etter landets lover. (You must abide by the laws of the land.)

gi etter (give in)

Du må ikke gi etter selv om de prøver å overtale deg. (You mustn't give in, even if they try to persuade you.)

skrive etter (send off for; type from)

Kan du skrive etter den boka for meg? (Can you send off for that book for me?)

Hun skriver etter diktat. (She types from dictation.)

ringe etter (telephone for)

Kan du ringe etter en drosje? (Can you phone for a taxi?)

være spørsmål etter (be in demand)

Det er ofte spørsmål etter den boka. (That book is often in demand.)

være ivrig etter (be eager, anxious to)

De er ivrige etter å lære så mye som mulig. (They are anxious to learn as much as possible.)

etter hva (from what)

Etter hva jeg har hørt, blir det ikke noe møte i dag. (From what I've heard, there won't be any meeting today.)

etter min mening (in my opinion)

Etter min mening er det for seint. (In my opinion, it's too late.)

alt etter som (according to)

Lett eller vanskelig, alt etter som man tar det. (Easy or difficult, according to how one takes it.)

alt etter (depending on)

Du kan velge mellom mange forskjellige tilbud alt etter hva du vil betale. (You can choose between lots of different offers, depending on what you want to pay.)

For

leve for (live for)
    Hun lever bare for sine barn. (She lives only for her children.)

presentere for (introduce to)
    Kan jeg få presentere deg for min kone? (May I introduce you to my wife?)

ha bruk for (need)
    Jeg har bruk for en sykkel. (I need a bicycle.)

grue for/til (dread)
    Jeg gruer (meg) for eksamen. (I'm dreading the exam.)

ha mulighet for (be capable of, have the possibility of)
    De bør ha mulighet for å ta lønnet arbeid. (They should have the possibility of taking paid work.)

vise interesse for (show an interest in)
    Hun viste interesse for innvandrerne. (She showed an interest in the immigrants.)

å være redd for (be afraid of; fear for)
    De er redd for det som er nytt og annerledes. (They are afraid of anything new and strange.)
    Hun er redd for sine barn. (a. She is afraid of her children; b. She fears for her children.)

ha behov for (be in need of, need)
    De har behov for å treffe andre mennesker. (They need to meet other people.)

bestemme seg for (decide)
    De har bestemt seg for å flytte. (They have decided to move house.)

kjempe for (fight for)
    De kjemper for friheten. (They are fighting for freedom.)

strever for (toil, struggle)
    Han strever for familien. (He toils for his family.)

forklare for (explain to)
    Han måtte forklare seg for politiet. (He had to explain himself to the police.)
    Kan du forklare dette for meg? (Can you explain this to me?)

vise forståelse for (sympathize with)
    Hun viste forståelse for deres problemer. (She sympathized with their problems.)

sørge for (support)
    Hun måtte sørge for barn og mann. (She had to support her children and husband.)

ha ansvar for (be responsible for)
Foreldrene har ansvar for barna sine. (Parents are responsible for their children.)
stemme for (vote in favour of, support)
Jeg stemmer for dette forslaget. (I vote in favour of this proposal.)
være glad for (be glad, happy)
Jeg er glad for at du kom. (I'm glad you came.)
til høyre for (to the right of)
Treet står til høyre for butikken. (The tree stands to the right of the shop.)
ta for seg (deal with, discuss)
Nå skal vi ta for oss denne boka. (We shall now deal with this book.)
foretrekke for (prefer to)
Han foretrekker vin for øl. (He prefers wine to beer.)
stå for tur (be someone's turn)
Hvem står for tur nå? (Whose turn is it now?)
Nå er det hennes tur. (Now it's her turn.)
nå for tiden (these days)
Nå for tiden er det dyrt å bygge. (These days, building is expensive.)
dag for dag (from one day to the next)
Det går bedre og bedre dag for dag. (Things keep getting better from one day to the next.)
for livet (for life; for one's life)
De har blitt venner for livet. (They have become friends for life.)
De løp for livet. (They ran for their lives.)
kjøpe for (buy for)
Han kjøpte eplet for to kroner. (He bought the apple for two kroner.)
Hun kjøpte melk for moren. (She bought milk for her mother.)
for det meste (for the most part)
Hun er for det meste hjemme. (She's at home for the most part.)
for . . . del (personally, for one's part)
Jeg for min del vil ikke gjøre det. (Personally, I wouldn't do that.)
være lett/vanskelig for (be easy/difficult for)
Det er ikke så lett for meg. (It's not that easy for me.)
Det er vanskelig for meg å lære norsk. (It's difficult for me to learn Norwegian.)

ha lett/vanskelig for (find it difficult)

Jeg har lett for å lære norsk. (I find it easy to learn Norwegian.)

være morsomt for (be fun for)

Det er morsomt for barna å gå på sirkus. (It's fun for the children to go to the circus.)

for en/et . . .! (What a . . .!)

For en dag! (What a day!)

For et svar! (What a strange answer!)

for det første (in the first place)

For det første var det kaldt ute, for det andre ville ikke bilen min gå. (In the first place, it was cold outside, and in the second place my car was broken down.)

ta for gitt (take for granted)

De tok det for gitt at de skulle få lån. (They took it for granted that they would get a loan.)

Fra

være unntak fra (be an exception to)

Dette er unntak fra regelen. (This is an exception to the rule.)

komme fra (come from; do (well, badly); escape)

Jeg kommer fra Italia. (I come from Italy.)

Han kom dårlig fra det. (He did badly; he made a bad job/mess of it.)

Han kom fra det med livet i behold. (He got out of it alive.)

høre fra (hear from)

Han har ikke hørt fra dem på to måneder. (He hasn't heard from them for two months.)

si fra (say so, let one know)

Kan du si fra når vi skal gå av bussen? (Can you let us know when to get off the bus?)

Si fra hvis det er noe dere ikke liker! (Say so if there's something you don't like!)

ta fra (take away, confiscate)

Politiet tok fra ham førerkortet fordi han kjørte for fort. (The police took away his driving licence because he was driving too fast.)

ta avstand fra (dissociate oneself from)

Han tok avstand fra landets politikk. (He dissociated himself from the country's politics.)

reise fra (travel from; leave)

Han reiste fra London til Oslo. (He travelled from London to Oslo.)

Han reiste fra familien. (He left his family.)

oversette fra (translate from)

Hun har oversatt den boka fra kinesisk. (She has translated that book from Chinese.)

fra før (from before, already)

Jeg vil ikke ha den boka for jeg har den fra før. (I don't want that book as I already have it.)

fra og med (f.o.m.) (starting from)

Fra og med i morgen åpner forretningen en halv time senere. (Starting tomorrow, the shop will open half an hour later.)

ta fra hverandre (take apart)

Han tok motoren fra hverandre og satte den sammen igjen. (He took the engine apart and put it back together again.)

bortsett fra (apart from)

Alle var til stede bortsett fra de to som måtte reise. (Everyone was there apart from the two who had to leave.)

være fra seg (be beside oneself, distraught)

Han var fra seg da han hadde mistet alle pengene sine. (He was beside himself when he lost all his money.)

fra eller til (more or less)

En krone fra eller til spiller ingen rolle. (One krone more or less doesn't matter.)

være forskjellig fra (be different from)

Norge er forskjellig fra andre land. (Norway is different from other countries.)

I

kle seg i (dress in)

Han kledde seg i sort. (He dressed in black.)

sette i gang (get started)

De satte i gang med én gang. (They got started straight away.)

være flink i (be good at)

Han er flink i gymnastikk. (He's good at gymnastics.)

være forelsket i (fall in love with)

Han ble forelsket i naboen sin. (He fell in love with his neighbour.)

være glad i (love, be fond of)

Han var glad i barna sine. (He loved his children.)

være interessert i (be interested in)

Hun er interessert i historie. (She is interested in history.)

være enig i (agree with)

Han var enig i det forslaget. (He agreed with that suggestion.)

gå i (be in; stick to; wear)

Han går i annen klasse. (He is in the second year at school.)

Det går i grønnsaker og ost. (We stick mostly to vegetables and cheese.)

Han går i bare skjorta. (He is only wearing a shirt.)

lese i (read in)

De leste i avisa at . . . (They read in the newspaper that . . .)

være noe i (be something in)

Det er noe i koppen. (There's something in the cup.)

Det er noe i det du sier. (There's something in what you say.)

inn i (into)

, Han gikk inn i huset. (He went into the house.)

gå i land (go ashore)

De gikk i land etter å ha seilt i to timer. (They went ashore after sailing for two hours.)

i god tid (in good time)

De kom i god tid. (They came in good time.)

i lengden (for any length of time, in the long run)

Det er kjedelig å spise poteter i lengden. (Eating potatoes for any length of time is boring.)

stå i (work; be registered at; be very busy)

Hun står i en forretning. (She works in a shop.)

Hun står i Oslo Trygdekasse. (She is registered at the Oslo Social Security Office.)

Han står i hele dagen. (He is very busy all day.)

i . . . vei/gate (in . . . road/street)

Jeg bor i Kirkeveien/Storgata. (I live in Church Road / High Street.)

være i arbeid (be working)

Han er i arbeid igjen etter ferien. (He's working again after the holidays.)

i god behold (safe and sound, in one piece)

Bagasjen kom fram i god behold. (The luggage arrived in one piece.)

i all hast / i full fart (in a hurry, at top speed)

Jeg gjorde det i all hast / i full fart. (I did it in a hurry.)

i det hele tatt (at all; altogether)

Han kom ikke i det hele tatt. (He didn't come at all.)

Det er i det hele tatt vanskelig å forstå dette. (It is altogether difficult to understand this.)

ha rett i (be right about)

Det har du rett i. (You're right about that.)

i praksis (in practice)

Det er vanskelig å gjennomføre det i praksis. (It's difficult to carry it out in practice.)

betale i (pay in; pay at)

Han betalt 40 % i skatt. (He paid 40 % tax.)

Han betalte i kroner, ikke i dollar. (He paid in kroner, not dollars.)

Han betalte i kassen. (He paid at the checkout.)

i norsk (in Norwegian)

I norsk er det mange vanskelige preposisjonsuttrykk. (There are many difficult prepositional phrases in Norwegian.)

But: Hvordan sier vi «merci», «thank you» *på* norsk? (How does one say «merci», «thank you» in Norwegian?)

i veien (wrong, the matter)

Hva er i veien med deg? (What's the matter with you?)

ha vondt i (have a pain, ache)

Jeg har vondt i hodet. (I have a headache.)

i leie (in rent)

Hun betaler 100 kr måneden i leie. (She pays 100 kroner a month in rent.)

kjøre i (drive at)

Han kjørte i 60. (He was driving at 60 kilometres an hour.)

Med

regne med (expect, count on, reckon on)

Jeg regner med at du kommer. (I reckon on you coming.)

drive med (be doing)

Hva driver du med for tiden? (What are you doing at present?)

sløse med (waste, squander)

De sløser med pengene. (They are wasting their money.)

snakke med (talk to)

Jeg skal snakke med naboen. (I'll talk to my neighbour.)

arbeide med (work on)

Jeg arbeider med planene. (I'm working on the plans.)

følge med (pay attention; go out with)

Nå må du følge godt med. (Now you must pay attention.)

Han har følge med ei norsk jente. (He is going out with a Norwegian girl.)

bry seg med (trouble, bother oneself with)

170

Ikke bry deg med dette! (Don't trouble yourself with that!)

føle med (sympathize with)

Jeg føler med deg. (I sympathize with you.)

være kjent med (be familiar with)

Er du kjent med reglene? (Are you familiar with the rules?)

være fornøyd med (be pleased, happy with)

Jeg er fornøyd med hybelen min. (I'm pleased with my lodgings.)

være sammen med (be with; be going out with)

Han er sammen med en norsk pike. (a. He's going out with a Norwegian girl. b. He's with a Norwegian girl.)

ha/ta med (have, take with)

Han tok med (seg) barna til byen. (He took the children (with him) to town.)

Hun hadde med seg mange penger på reisen. (She had a lot of money with her on her trip.)

være enig med (agree with)

Jeg er enig med deg. (I agree with you.)

bli med / være med (go/come with)

Vil du bli/være med meg på kino? (Do you want to come/go to the cinema with me?)

sammen med (with)

Han bor sammen med foreldrene sine. (He lives with his parents.)

være ferdig med (have finished)

Jeg er ferdig med oppgaven. (I've finished the exercise.)

gå med (accept, agree to; be consumed, go; wear)

Jeg kan gå med på det. (I can accept that.)

All maten har gått med. (All the food has gone.)

Hva skal du gå med i kveld? (What are you going to wear this evening?)

være med (go along on, be part of)

Han er med på en reise til Kanariøyene. (He went along on a trip to the Canary Islands.)

ta det med ro (take it easy)

Nå skal vi ta det med ro et par dager. (Now we'll take it easy for a couple of days.)

til og med (until, up to and including)

Han skal være der til og med søndag. (He'll be there until Sunday.)

hjelpe med (help with)

Kan du hjelpe meg med dette? (Can you help me with this?)

Mellom

forskjellen mellom (the difference between)
Hva er forskjellen mellom «både» og «begge»? (What is the difference between «både» and «begge»?)

lese mellom linjene (read between the lines)
Her kan man lese mye mellom linjene. (One can read a lot between the lines here.)

bli mellom (be between)
Dette får bli mellom oss. (Let's keep this between ourselves.)

snakke seg i mellom (talk to each other, talk between themselves)
De snakker seg i mellom på norsk. (They speak to each other in Norwegian.)
De snakker norsk seg i mellom. (They speak Norwegian between themselves.)

Mot

kjempe mot (fight against)
Han kjempet mot fienden. (He fought against the enemy.)

være hyggelig mot (be pleasant towards)
De er så hyggelige mot meg. (They're so pleasant towards me.)

være snill mot (be kind to)
Du må være snill mot dyra. (You must be kind to the animals.)

være slem mot (be mean, cruel to)
Han var slem mot dyra. (He was cruel to the animals.)

gjøre motstand mot (resist, oppose)
De gjorde motstand mot fienden. (They resisted the enemy.)

spille mot (play against)
Norge spilte mot Nederland i den fotballkampen. (Norway played against the Netherlands in that football match.)

være mot (be against, oppose)
Han er mot utbygging av kjernekraft. (He opposes the development of nuclear power.)

gå mot (cross on)
Du må ikke gå mot rødt lys. (You musn't cross the street on a red light.)

vindu mot (window looking out on)
Jeg har vindu mot gata. (I have a window looking out on the street.)

mot jul/vinter/vår (approaching Christmas/winter/spring)
Det går mot jul. (Christmas is approaching.)

vedta mot (accepted against)

Forslaget ble vedtatt mot tre stemmer. (The proposal was accepted with three votes against.)

mot slutten (towards the end)

Det går mot slutten nå. (The end is getting near.)

Mot slutten av året skal vi ha ferie. (We are going on holiday towards the end of the year.)

Om

spørre om (ask)

Kan du spørre om veien? (Can you ask the way?)

be om (ask for)

Hun ber om et glass vann. (She asks for a glass of water.)

Hun ber om unnskyldning. (She apologizes; lit.: asks for forgiveness.)

synes om (think of; like)

Hva synes du om norsk mat? (What do you think of Norwegian food?)

Jeg synes om henne. (I like her.)

være overbevist om (be convinced)

Jeg er overbevist om at det ikke går. (I'm convinced it won't work.)

snakke om (talk about)

De snakker om været. (They are talking about the weather.)

Du snakker om! (Good grief!)

fortelle om (talk, tell about)

Han fortalte om familien sin. (He talked about his family.)

skrive om (write about; rewrite)

Han skrev om sitt liv. (He wrote about his life.)

Du må skrive om denne setningen. (a. You must write about this sentence; b. You must rewrite this sentence.)

lese om (read about)

Jeg har lest om det i avisa. (I have read about it in the paper.)

kjempe om (fight for)

De kjemper om de første plassene. (They are fighting for the first places.)

konkurrere om (compete for)

De konkurrerer om de første plassene. (They are competing for the first places.)

tenke om (think about)

Hva tenker du om det? (What do you think about that?)

mene om / tro om (think about)

Hva mener/tror du om det? (What do you think about that?)
bry seg om (be bothered about)
Han bryr seg ikke om det. (He isn't bothered about that.)
om igjen (again, once more)
Si det om igjen! (Say it again!)
om og men (ifs and buts)
Det var så mye om og men. (There were so many ifs and buts.)

Over
tenke over (think about)
Du må tenke over disse spørsmålene. (You must think about these questions.)
regne over (go over the figures)
Jeg skal regne over og se om jeg har råd. (I'll go over the figures and see if I can afford it.)
bestemme over (decide over, control)
Foreldrene vil gjerne bestemme over barna. (The parents want to control the children.)
sette over (put on)
Sett over kaffekjelen! (Put the coffee on!)
ta over (take over)
Han skal ta over etter meg. (He will take over from me.)
komme over (come across; get over)
Hvis du kommer over noen antikviteter, er jeg interessert i å kjøpe dem. (If you come across any antiques I'm interested in buying them.)
Han kom ikke over det. (He didn't get over it.)
Han kom over på den andre siden. (He got across to the other side.)
ha oversikt over (have in order, have a good idea of)
Jeg har oversikt over økonomien. (I have my finances in order.)
være klar over (be aware of)
Jeg er klar over problemene. (I am aware of the problems.)
være imponert over (be impressed by)
Han er imponert over dem. (He is impressed by them.)
være overrasket over (be surprised at)
Jeg er overrasket over de høye prisene i Norge. (I am surprised at the high prices in Norway.)
skuffet over (be disappointed in/by)
Han var skuffet over middagen. (He was disappointed by the dinner.)

gå over (pass; cross over; check)

    Det går nok over. (I'm sure it'll pass.)

    Han gikk over gata. (He crossed the street.)

    Han måtte gå over regnskapet. (He had to check the accounts.)

På

gå på (go to; keep it up)

    Gå på kino. (Go to the cinema.)

    Bare gå på! (Just keep it up!)

gå med på (accept, agree to)

    Jeg kan gå med på det. (I can accept that.)

stå på (be on; stick to one's guns)

    Radioen står på – skru den av, vær så snill! (The radio is on – turn it off, please!)

    Bare stå på! (Just stick to your guns!)

ha penger på seg (have money on one)

    Har du noen penger på deg? (Do you have any money on you?)

ta på (touch; put on; get one down)

    Han tok på den varme kjelen og brant seg. (He touched the hot saucepan and burned himself.)

    Ta på deg denne jakken! (Put this jacket on!)

    Alt dette arbeidet tar på. (All this work gets you down.)

vente på (wait for)

    Han ventet på trikken. (He waited for the tram.)

ha lyst på (want, would like)

    Jeg har lyst på en kopp kaffe. (I would like a cup of coffee.)

høre på (listen to)

    Vil du høre på meg litt? (Will you listen to me for a minute?)

rope på (call)

    Kan du rope på Anne? (Can you call Anne?)

finne på (be up to)

    Hva er det du finner på? (What are you up to?)

komme på (come to; remember)

    Hvor mye blir det? Det kommer på tre kroner. (How much is it? It comes to three kroner.)

    Jeg kan ikke komme på hva hun heter. (I can't remember her name.)

passe på (look after)

    Kan du passe på veska mi? (Can you look after my bag?)

lure på (wonder)

    Jeg lurer på om det blir regn. (I wonder if it'll rain.)

tenke på (think of)

Jeg tenker på deg. (I'm thinking of you.)

tvile på (doubt)

Jeg tviler på at det går. (I doubt that will work.)

hilse på (greet, meet)

Har du hilst på sønnen min? (Have you met my son?)

se på (look at)

Har du sett på de bildene? (Have you looked at those pictures?)

synes synd på (feel sorry for)

Han syntes synd på de syke barna. (He felt sorry for the sick children.)

på norsk (in Norwegian)

Kan du si dette på norsk? (Can you say this in Norwegian?)

gang på gang (time and time again)

Hun sa det gang på gang. (She said it time and time again.)

bo på (live in)

Hun bor på hybel / på hotell. (She lives in lodgings / in a hotel.)

Hun bor på tre rom og kjøkken. (She lives in a two-bedroomed flat.)

NB! Hun bor *i* en leilighet / et hus / tredje etasje. (She lives in a flat / in a house / on the third floor.)

svare på (answer)

Kan du svare på dette spørsmålet? (Can you answer this question?)

forskjell på (a difference between)

Det er forskjell på rik og fattig. (There's a difference between the rich and the poor.)

forskjellen på (the difference between)

Hva er forskjellen på rik og fattig? (What is the difference between rich and poor?)

sikker på (sure)

Jeg er sikker på at hun kommer. (I'm sure she'll come.)

eksempel på (example of)

Kan du gi meg et eksempel på det? (Can you give me an example of that?)

pris på (price of)

Hva er prisen på gulrøttene? (What price are the carrots?)

være spent på (be anxious, curious to know)

Jeg er spent på om han kommer. (I'm anxious to know whether he will come.)

gjøre inntrykk på (make an impression on)

De sultne barna gjorde sterkt inntrykk på oss. (The starving children made a deep impression on us.)

være med på (take part in, be involved in)

Han er med på mye rart. (He is involved in all sorts of things.)

Til

være nødt til (to have to, be obliged to)

Du er nødt til å gjøre det. (You have to do it.)

ha tid til (have time)

Jeg har ikke tid til å snakke med deg. (I haven't got time to talk to you.)

ha anledning til (be able to, be in a position to)

Han har ikke anledning til å komme i dag. (He isn't able to come today.)

adressen til (the address of)

Adressen til det firmaet er . . . (The address of that company is . . .)

ha mulighet til (be able, have the possibility of)

Han har ikke mulighet til å komme i dag. (He isn't able to come today.)

ha sjanse(n) til (have the chance to)

Nå har du sjanse(n) til å snakke norsk. (Now you have the chance to speak Norwegian.)

ha kjennskap til (know something about)

Har du noe kjennskap til dette? (Do you know anything about this?)

ha evne til (possess the ability to)

Han har ikke evne til å forstå det. (He doesn't possess the ability to understand that.)

ha lyst til (would like to)

Jeg har lyst til å gjøre det. (I would like to do it.)

til frokost (for breakfast)

Hva skal vi ha til frokost? (What shall we have for breakfast?)

ringe til (ring, call)

Kan du ringe henne etter kl 3? (Can you ring her after 3 o'clock?)

si til (tell)

Si til henne at jeg skal komme i morgen. (Tell her I'll come tomorrow.)

be til (invite to; pray to)

Jeg er bedt til middag til noen venner. (I have been invited to some friends for dinner.)

Jeg ber til Gud. (I pray to God.)

glede seg til (look forward to)

Jeg gleder meg til jul. (I am looking forward to Christmas.)

venne seg til (get used to)

Du må venne deg til den norske maten hvis du skal bo her. (You will have to get used to Norwegian food if you are going to live here.)

lykke til! (good luck!)

Lykke til med arbeidet! (Good luck with your work!)

være vant til (be used to)

Jeg er ikke vant til den norske maten! (I'm not used to Norwegian food!)

få lov til (be allowed to)

Han fikk ikke lov til å reise. (He wasn't allowed to go.)

være flink til (be good, gifted at)

Hun er flink til å spille piano. (She's good at playing the piano.)

være til nytte (be of use)

Reglene var til ingen nytte. (The rules were of no use.)

være til hjelp (be of help)

Grammatikken var til stor hjelp for meg. (The grammar was a great help to me.)

føre til (lead to, result in)

Det førte til at hun ble syk. (It resulted in her falling ill.)

passe til (fit)

Kjolen passet til henne. (The dress fit her.)

stå til (be feeling; take its course; go with, match)

Hvordan står det til? (How are you?)

Det får stå til. (It will have to take its course.)

Fargene står til hverandre. (The colours go well with each other.)

høre til (belong to, be a part of)

Finnmark hører til Norge. (Finnmark is a part of Norway.)

grue til (dread)

Jeg gruer meg til eksamen. (I'm dreading the exam(s).)

ha til gode (have due, owing)

Jeg har 50 kroner til gode. (I have 50 kroner due to me.)

til slutt (finally, in the end)

Til slutt måtte hun gå og legge seg. (In the end she had to go to bed.)

til jul (for Christmas)

Hva fikk du til jul? (What did you get for Christmas?)

én til (one more, another one)

Først kom det én bil og så én til. (First one car came, then another.)

søsteren til (sister of)

Det er søsteren til moren hans. (That's his mother's sister.)

II Sentence Elements

Subject

Example:
Peter kommer fra England. (Peter comes from England.)
↑
SUBJECT

Who comes from England? Answer: Peter.

Bilen kjører fort. (The car is going fast.)
↑
SUBJECT

What is going fast? Answer: the car.

The subject of a clause can usually be identified by asking the
question «Who?» or «What?» followed by the verb phrase.

«DET» AS SUBJECT
a. Examples:
  1. *Det* bor mange utlendinger i Norge. (There are many
     foreigners living in Norway.)
  2. *Det* står en kopp på bordet. (There is a cup on the table.)
  3. Her har *det* stått et tre. (There has been a tree standing here.)
  4. På den andre siden av veien lå *det* en butikk. (On the other
     side of the road there used to be a shop.)

In the sentences above, «det» is the grammatical subject
although we know that the real subject is:
1. mange utlendinger (many foreigners)
2. en kopp (a cup)
3. et tre (a tree)
4. en butikk (a shop)

«Det» corresponds here to the English «there» followed by a part of the verb «to be». This construction only occurs in Norwegian when the real subject is a noun phrase in the indefinite form. However, it is a usage which is preferred in many contexts. It is, though, also quite acceptable to say:

1. Mange utlendinger bor i Norge. (Many foreigners live in Norway.)
2. En kopp står på bordet. (A cup is on the table.)
3. Et tre har stått her. (A tree has stood here.)
4. En butikk lå på den andre siden av veien. (A shop used to be on the other side of the road.)

Note that in the Norwegian construction corresponding to existential «there» + the verb «to be» + the 'real' subject in the indefinite form, «det» cannot normally be dropped.
Example:
På den andre siden av veien var *det* en butikk. (On the other side of the road there used to be a shop.)

Wrong: På den andre siden av veien var en butikk. En butikk var på den andre siden av veien.

b. Examples:
Det regner. (It's raining.)
I Norge er *det* kaldt. (It's cold in Norway.)
Det banker på døra. (Someone is knocking on the door.)
Det gikk bra. (It went well.)

«Det» here is the formal subject, usually equivalent to the «empty» subject *it* in English, and no other subject occurs in the clause.

Verb Phrase

Example:
Linda *leser* avisa. (Linda is reading the paper.)
     ↑
VERB PHRASE

What is Linda doing? Answer: Reading.

181

VERB PHRASE

Han *har* allerede *arbeidet* der i tjue år.
(He has already worked there for twenty years.)

What has he done? Answer: Worked.

The verb phrase can usually be identified by asking what the subject of the clause is doing.

Complement

THE SUBJECT COMPLEMENT
Example:
Hun er *veldig gammel.* (She is very old.)
↑
COMPLEMENT

What is she? Answer: Very old.

Datteren hennes heter *Maria.* (Her daughter is called Maria.)
↑
COMPLEMENT

What is she called? Answer: Maria.

Han ser *fin* ut. (He looks well.)
↑
COMPLEMENT

How does he look? Answer: Well.

The subject complement of a clause can normally be found by asking: how is? + the subject.

Verbs such as «hete» (be called), «være» (be), «kalles» (be called), «bli» (become), «se ut» (look), «føle seg» (feel), etc. are dependent verbs, and as such cannot occur on their own – they must be followed by another sentence element. This element is called the complement.

Wrong: Datteren hennes heter. Hun er.

Note, however, that the verbs «føle seg» and «se ut» can in certain contexts be used independently, particularly in idiomatic constructions.
Examples:
Han ser ikke ut! (He looks dreadful!)
Han føler seg nå. (Now he has a high opinion of himself.)

THE OBJECT COMPLEMENT
Examples:
Han malte huset *rødt*. (He painted the house red.)
                  ↑
    (OBJECT) COMPLEMENT

Han lakkerte bilen *rød*. (He sprayed the car red.)
                ↑
    (OBJECT) COMPLEMENT

Hun skjenket glassene *fulle*. (She filled up the glasses.)
                ↑
    (OBJECT) COMPLEMENT

De fant husene *tomme*. (They found the houses empty.)
                ↑
    (OBJECT) COMPLEMENT

Jeg føler meg *dum*. (I feel stupid.)
             ↑
    (OBJECT) COMPLEMENT

The object complement can often be found by asking «How is/are?» + the object.
The object complement agrees with the object in number and gender.

COMPLEMENT IN SET PHRASES
Examples:
De var *glad* i hverandre. (They were fond of each other.)
De holdt pengene *klar(e)*. (They held their money ready.)
Han slapp oksene *løs*. (He turned the bulls loose.)

In set phrases like these the complement often remains uninflected.
See also the section on Adjectives.

183

FREE COMPLEMENT

Examples:

Trøtt og sliten fortsatte han arbeidet. (Tired and weary, he went on with the work.)

Trøtte og slitne satte de seg ned. (Tired and weary, they sat down.)

Tjue år gammel giftet han seg. (He got married at twenty.)

Sju år gamle begynner de på skolen. (They start school at the age of seven.)

Som barn var jeg ofte syk. (As a child, I was often ill.)

Free complements are more loosely attached to the subject, but still inflect for number and gender.

Object

Example:

Marie kjøpte *et stort eple*. (Marie bought a large apple.)
         ↑
     OBJECT

What did she buy? Answer: A large apple.

The object is found by asking «What?» or «Who?» + verb + subject.

Indirect Object

Example:

Marie gav *meg* et eple. (Marie gave me an apple.)
         ↑
 INDIRECT OBJECT

To whom did she give an apple? Answer: To me.

Han gjorde *meg* en tjeneste. (He did me a favour.)
          ↑
  INDIRECT OBJECT

For whom did he do a favour? Answer: For me.

The indirect object can usually be identified by asking «To»/«For whom?» + verb + subject + object.

Adverbial

The adverbial can be:

a. **a prepositional phrase:**
   Examples:
   Jeg bor *i Norge*. (I live in Norway.)
         ↑
        ADVERBIAL

   I morgen skal vi ta en tur *til byen*.
     ↑   ↑
   ADVERBIAL   ADVERBIAL

   (Tomorrow we'll go into town.)

b. **an adverb:**
   Examples:
   Her bor jeg. (I live here.)
   ↑
   ADVERBIAL

   Hun går *raskt*. (She walks fast.)
        ↑
       ADVERBIAL

   De kommer *alltid for sent*. (They always come late.)
            ↑
          ADVERBIAL

c. **an adverb of place:** (see also a.)
   Example:
   De kjørte *denne veien*. (They drove this way.)
          ↑
        ADVERBIAL

d. **an adverbial phrase of time:**
   Example:
   Hver gang jeg får et brev, blir jeg glad.
      ↑
   ADVERBIAL
   (Every time I get a letter I'm happy.)

e. **an adverbial phrase of measurement:**
   Example:
   Han gikk *to kilometer*. (He walked two kilometres.)
          ↑
        ADVERBIAL

185

III Sentence Structure

Main Clauses

Examples:
Per skriver. (Per is writing.)
Per skriver et brev. (Per is writing a letter.)
I dag skriver Per et brev. (Today Per is writing a letter.)
Skriver Per et brev? (Is Per writing a letter?)
Hva gjør Per? (What is Per doing?)
Han skriver et brev hjem. (He is writing a letter home.)
Skriv! (Write!)

A main clause can stand alone and have complete meaning. This is not the case for a subordinate clause.

Subordinate Clauses

Examples:

«THAT»-CLAUSES
Han sa *at han skulle komme.* (He said that he was going to come.)

RELATIVE CLAUSES
Mannen *som står der,* er broren min. (The man who is standing there is my brother.)

INTERROGATIVE CLAUSES
Han spurte *om jeg ville komme.* (He asked if I wanted to come.)
Jeg vet ikke *hvor de bor.* (I don't know where they live.)
Vet du *hva han heter?* (Do you know his name?)

ADVERBIAL CLAUSES
(introduced by a subordinating conjunction):
Jeg må ta på meg jakke *fordi det er kaldt.* (I must put a jacket on because it's cold.)

Da han kom, gikk vi. (When he came, we left.)
Hvis du vil, kan jeg hjelpe deg. (If you want, I can help you.)
Selv om han ikke er norsk, snakker han norsk. (Although he isn't Norwegian, he speaks Norwegian.)

A subordinate clause cannot stand alone and give complete meaning. It must be attached to a main clause.

IV Word Order

Main Clauses

THE POSITION OF THE SUBJECT

a. The subject is often placed first in a main clause.
Examples:

1	2		
Han	ville	komme.	(He wanted to come.)
Jeg	snakker	norsk.	(I speak Norwegian.)
De	vil	ikke reise ennå.	(They don't want to leave yet.)

b. However, the main clause can also begin with other parts of speech, often to give them added emphasis:
Examples:

1	2	3		
I morgen	blir	det	nok pent vær.	(Tomorrow it will probably be fine weather.)
Henne	liker	jeg	godt.	(I like her very much.)
Nå	kan	jeg	snakke litt norsk.	(Now I can speak some Norwegian.)
Trikken	tar	de	hver dag.	(They take the tram every day.)

Whenever the main clause begins with a part of speech other than the subject, the order of the subject and verb is reversed (inversion). The subject then occurs as the third element of the clause.

THE POSITION OF THE VERB PHRASE
(present and past tense forms) always comes second in a main clause. (In questions which are not introduced by an interrogative, the first position is empty).

188

Examples:

1	2		
Han	kommer	nå.	(He is coming now.)
Nå	kommer	han.	(Now he is coming.)
I morgen	skal	vi synge.	(Tomorrow we are going to sing.)
Jeg	har	aldri truffet ham.	(I have never met him.)
	Kommer	han snart?	(Is he coming soon?)
	Snakker	du norsk?	(Do you speak Norwegian?)

THE POSITION OF THE ADVERBIAL PHRASE

a. **The adverbial phrase can occupy various positions in a main clause.**

Examples:

1	2	3	4 *Adverbial*		*Adverbial*	
Nå	kan	du	ikke	komme	til meg.	(You can't come to see me now.)
Hun	kan		også	synge	veldig fint.	(She sings very well too.)
Disse	plantene	vokser			bra overalt.	(These plants grow well everywhere.)
Eplet	har	han	allerede	gitt	til henne.	(He has already given the apple to her.)
	Kommer	du	snart?			(Are you coming soon?)
Kaffe	drikker	de	alltid		i Norge.	(They always drink coffee in Norway.)
			sjelden (seldom)		der. (there)	
			faktisk (in fact)		om morgenen. (in the morning)	
			vanligvis (usually)		hver dag. (every day)	
			jo (really)		til frokost. (for breakfast)	
			nok (probably)		kl 8.00. (at 8 a.m.)	
			gjerne (preferably)		på fest. (at a party.)	
			ofte (often)		i restauranten. (at the restaurant)	
			sikkert (I'm sure)		hjemme hver dag. (at home every day)	
			vel/da (I imagine)		ute nå. (outside now)	

190

b. **Adverbial phrases such as those in final position in the examples above can also come at the beginning of a main clause. The same applies to certain of the adverbs in fourth place above.**
Examples:

1				
I Norge	drikker	de	kaffe.	(In Norway they drink coffee.)
Ofte				(Often . . .)
Hver dag				(Every day . . .)
Vanligvis				(Usually . . .)

c. **In sentences containing both an adverbial phrase of place and an adverbial phrase of time, the latter is usually placed last when both come at the end of the sentence:**
Examples:

		Adv. of place	Adv. of time	
De drikker	kaffe	hjemme	hver dag.	(They drink coffee at home every day.)
Hun tar	bussen	til kontoret	kl 8.00.	(She takes the bus to the office at 8 a.m.)
De vil	spise	ute	i dag.	(They want to eat out today.)

d. **The other adverbs, such as «ikke», «også», «alltid» and so on, usually come in fourth place in the sentence.**

e. **However, if the subject of the sentence is a noun or a proper name, the adverbial phrase is normally placed in front of the subject, ie. in third place.**
Examples:

1	2	3 Adv.	4 Subject		
Nå	kan	ikke	mannen	komme.	(Now the man can't come.)
Her	vil	nok	Marie	bo.	(Marie will no doubt want to live here.)
Eplet	har	visst	Peter	gitt henne.	(I think Peter has given her the apple.)
Kaffe	drikker	vel	nordmenn	hver dag?	(Norwegians drink coffee every day, don't they?)
	Kommer	ikke	barna	til middag?	(Aren't the children coming to dinner?)

191

f. **The same sentence structure can be used to give particular emphasis to the subject pronoun:**
Examples:

1	2	3 Adv.	4 Subject		
Nå	kan	ikke	du	komme, bare de andre.	(Now *you* can't come, only the others.)
I Norge	må	også	vi	betale skatt, ikke bare nordmennene.	(In Norway we have to pay tax too, not just the Norwegians.)
Dette	kan	vel	jeg	gjøre?	(Surely I can do this?)

POSITION OF THE DIRECT AND INDIRECT OBJECT
Examples:

	Indirect obj.	Direct obj.		
Han har gitt	meg	en blomst.		(He has given me a flower.)
Han har gitt	meg	den.		(He has given it to me.)
De sendte	ham	et brev.		(They sent him a letter.)
De sendte	ham	det.		(They sent it to him.)
De sendte	mannen	et brev.		(They sent the man a letter.)
De sendte	John	et brev.		(They sent John a letter.)
But note:				
De sendte		det	til mannen.	(They sent it to the man.)
De sendte		det	til John.	(They sent it to John.)

The indirect object is always placed in front of the direct object. When the indirect object is a proper noun such as «John», or a noun, such as «the man», it is usually included in a prepositional phrase («til mannen» (to the man) / «til John» (to John)), which is placed after the direct object.

POSITION OF THE REFLEXIVE PRONOUN
Examples:

Her	har	han	ikke	likt *seg*.		(He hasn't
Han	har		ikke	likt *seg*	her.	liked it here.)
Her	vil	han	nok	like *seg*.		(I'm sure he'll
Han	vil		nok	like *seg*	her.	like it here.)
Han	likte	*seg*	ikke	her.		(He didn't like
Her	likte	han	*seg*	ikke.		it here.)

Wrong: Han likte ikke seg her. Her likte han ikke seg.

As a general rule it is useful to remember that the reflexive pronoun immediately follows the main verb, though bearing in mind that the reflexive pronoun cannot come before the subject.
Example:
Her likte han seg.

Wrong: «Her likte seg han»

Note also the position of the reflexive pronoun in a verb phrase consisting of verb + particle:
å ta av *seg* (to take off)
Han tok ikke av *seg* frakken. (He didn't take off his coat.)
Her tok han ikke av *seg* frakken. (He didn't take off his coat here.)

å ta *seg* av (to take care of)
Han tok *seg* ikke av moren sin. (He didn't take care of his mother.)
I flere år tok han *seg* ikke av moren sin. (For several years he didn't take care of his mother.)

Subordinate clauses

Examples:

1 Conjunction	2 Subject	3 Adverbial	4 Verb phrase		
. . . (at)	han	ikke	har vært	her på lenge.	(. . . that he hasn't been here for ages.)
. . . fordi	de	også	ville ha	ferie.	(. . .because they wanted to have a holiday too.)
Hvis	dere	alltid	snakker	engelsk . . .	(If you always speak English . . .)
. . . (som)	de	ikke	kunne bruke	i Norge.	(. . . (that) they couldn't use in Norway.)
. . . hvor	de	alltid	bodde	om sommeren.	(. . . where they always stayed in the summer.)
Da	jeg		var	barn, . . .	(When I was a child, . . .)

The structure of subordinate clauses is more rigid than that of main clauses. The following rules apply:

First place:　conjunction/relative pronoun/interrogative («at» (that) and «som» (which) can sometimes be omitted – see the sections on Conjunctions and Relative pronouns).

Second place:　subject
Third place:　adverbial phrase
Fourth place:　the entire verb phrase
Remaining places: the same rules apply as for main clauses.

Subordinate Clause relative to Main Clause

SUBORDINATE CLAUSE FIRST
Examples:

Subordinate clause	Main clause	
Hvis du snakker engelsk,	forstår jeg deg ikke.	(If you speak English I can't understand you.)
Når de kommer hjem,	skal de få mat.	(When they come home they'll get something to eat.)
Selv om det regner ute,	vil jeg gå en tur.	(Even though it's raining outside I want to go for a walk.)
Fordi han ikke kom,	kunne vi ikke reise.	(Because he didn't come, we couldn't leave.)

When a subordinate clause precedes a main clause, the verb always comes first in the main clause. In order to remember this, try to imagine that the whole subordinate clause occupies the first position in the main clause.

MAIN CLAUSE FIRST
When the main clause precedes a subordinate clause, there is no change in the standard word order.

Examples:

Main clause	Subordinate clause	Main clause	
Han skal komme hit	hvis du vil.		
	Hvis du vil,	skal han komme hit.	(He'll come here if you like.)
Hun vet	hva du heter.		
	Hva du heter,	vet hun.	(She knows what your name is.)
De liker seg ute	når det snør.		
	Når det snør,	liker de seg ute.	(They like it outside when it snows.)
Note also:			
Hvor bor du?			(Where do you live?)
Han spør	hvor du bor.		(He is asking where you live.)
Hva heter du?			(What is your name?)
Han spør	hva du heter.		(He is asking what your name is.)
Kommer du?			(Are you coming?)
Han spør	om du kommer.		(He is asking whether you are coming.)

Rules for the use of commas

A comma is obligatory

1. **when a subordinate clause precedes a main clause:**
   Hvis du vil, kan jeg hjelpe deg. (If you want, I can help you.)

2. **when a main clause is followed by a non-restrictive subordinate clause which basically acts as a parenthesis:**
   Hun snakket med foreldrene sine, som nettopp hadde kommet hjem fra ferie. (She spoke to her parents, who had just come back from their holiday.)

3. **when a subordinate clause acts as an appositive:**
   Hun ville be Kari, som er fire år, til fødselsdagen sin. (She wanted to invite Kari, who is four years old, to her birthday party.)

   Note that when a subordinate clause is inserted in a main clause, there is only a comma *after* the former, and not before:
   Hansen som står der, er seksti år i dag. (Hansen, who is standing there, is sixty today.)

4. **with appositives which are not subordinate clauses:**
   Katrine, vår yngste datter, er veldig glad i katter. (Katrine, our youngest daughter, loves cats.)

5. **in enumeration:**
   Han skulle kjøpe egg, brød, ost og melk. (He was going to buy eggs, bread, cheese and milk.)

6. **between two sentences connected by a coordinating conjunction («og», «eller», «for», «men»):**
   Hun spurte om de ville arbeide i dag, eller om de ville ha fri. (She asked them if they wanted to work today, or if they wanted to have the day off.)

   However, a comma is usually dropped in this category if both sentences are very short
   Barna sov og foreldrene arbeidet. (The children slept and the parents worked.)

7. **after mild interjections, responses and terms of address:**
   Uff, så kaldt der er! (Ugh, it's so cold!)
   Ja, nå går det bra. (Yes, now it's all right.)
   Kari, kom hit! (Kari, come here!)

8. **following direct speech:**
   «Det står bra til med oss,» svarte hun. («Everything's fine with us», she replied.)

INDEX

197

201